KARMA

T0312887

KARMA

WHY EVERYTHING YOU
KNOW ABOUT IT IS WRONG

ACHARYA
PRASHANT

PENGUIN BOOKS
An imprint of Penguin Random House

PENGUIN BOOKS

USA | Canada | UK | Ireland | Australia
New Zealand | India | South Africa | China | Singapore

Penguin Books is part of the Penguin Random House group of companies
whose addresses can be found at global.penguinrandomhouse.com

Published by Penguin Random House India Pvt. Ltd
4th Floor, Capital Tower 1, MG Road,
Gurugram 122 002, Haryana, India

First published in Penguin Books by Penguin Random House India 2021

Copyright © Acharya Prashant 2021

All rights reserved

10 9 8 7 6 5 4 3 2

The views and opinions expressed in this book are the author's own and the
facts are as reported by him which have been verified to the extent possible,
and the publishers are not in any way liable for the same.

ISBN 9780143453314

Typeset in Minion Pro by Manipal Technologies Limited, Manipal
Printed at Manipal Technologies Limited, India

This book is sold subject to the condition that it shall not, by way of trade
or otherwise, be lent, resold, hired out, or otherwise circulated without the
publisher's prior consent in any form of binding or cover other than that in
which it is published and without a similar condition including this condition
being imposed on the subsequent purchaser.

www.penguin.co.in

This is a legitimate digitally printed version of the book and therefore might not
have certain extra finishing on the cover.

Contents

PART III: ACTION THAT REFORMS THE ACTOR

PART IV: WHAT DO THE SCRIPTURES SAY?

About the Book

This book was spoken first and written later.

As a Vedanta philosopher and teacher, Acharya Prashant has been interacting with diverse audiences for over a decade. Though the questioners come from varying backgrounds, each of these interactions is usually in the form of a question that the teacher responds to. The length of each such interaction varies from ten minutes to as much as an hour. Every chapter of this book is essentially based on one such interaction. This means that each chapter, though coming from a single centre, exhibits the response of the speaker to very different people and their life-queries. The questioners are spaced apart across years, continents, genders, and everything else that makes a human being diverse from the other. This means that the readers get an enriching kaleidoscopic perspective as they go through the range of human conditions, confusions and questions – all related to the question of one's identity, which, as we shall learn in the book, is central to the question of the how to take the right action.

Karma is a word as common in the spiritual lexicon as in the popular parlance. However, its real meaning and implications stand obfuscated and distorted by centuries of misplaced expositions and self-appeasing translations. While commoners console themselves with the pedestrian notions attached to this word, it remains a disquieting enigma to those who refuse to resort to easy versions of the truth. This book is for the latter.

Moment by moment, life is synonymous with action. If to live rightly is to act rightly, then what is the right action? This has tormented human consciousness since ages.

The scriptures have tried to classically answer this question, but scriptures are infamous for being cryptic. They do not stoop to edify us with elaborations and examples, nor do they exactly advise how their ancient words apply to the current times. It is at this point that Acharya Prashant's exegesis and elucidations provide the missing link. In the ever-growing jungle of neo-spiritual illusions, the author provides clear-sighted guidance, addressing the most essential aspect of our life from a point of unified understanding and realization. The consequent decision-making leads directly to earnest and fearless action.

The book proceeds by demolishing the most prevalent myths regarding action, decision, and work by bringing the focus on the actor, rather than the action. From the darkness of confusion when we want to ask, 'What to do?' the book handholds us into the light of the question, 'Who is the doer? What does he want from the deed?' This transformation of investigation provides all the solutions, and finally the dissolution of the question itself.

The centuries-old widely prevalent myths related to Karma are peddled by ignorance or self-interest, or both. This book bombards the high palaces of dark and ubiquitous authority, and when they come crashing down, we discover they never had any scriptural foundations at all.

This is a work to be met not with the armours of our deep beliefs, but bare-chested, like a lover. If you are someone with the courage to challenge the tyrannies of tradition, authority and obscurantism, and the love to greet the naked truth, this book is for you, and only for you.

A word of caution: Because of the vast differences among seekers and their queries, the responses of the teacher too are customized and not standardized. At some places, therefore, the responses in one chapter may appear to be apparently contradictory to the responses in another chapter. We hope that our discrete readers will be able to appreciate the differences as the various roads leading to the same core.

Acharya Prashant

The Vedas are the oldest religious documents known to man. And Vedanta is the crown jewel, the absolute peak, of the Vedic essence.

The world today finds itself grappling with problems unseen in history. The problems of the past were mostly related to poverty, disease, hunger, illiteracy, lack of knowledge, and lack of technology. In short, the challenge was external, the enemy—whether in the form of a microbe or lack of resources—was outside. It was about man struggling against the tyranny of his external circumstances.

The last hundred years have been, however, different. And the current century has raised the spectre of man's conflicts to a very different and difficult theatre. The secrets of the atom and the universe have more or less yielded to man's relentless investigation. Poverty, illiteracy and disease are no more the invincible monsters they used to be. Today, matter is at man's beck and call, and there is ambition to colonise the universe, and even beat death.

It should then sound like the best of times. The current period should be the best one in the history of our species. Far from that, we find ourselves staring at, as we said, a very different dimension of challenge in the inner theatre. Having conquered almost everything in the external world, man finds he is today a bigger slave to himself than he ever was. And it's an ignominious slavery—to rule all, only to find that inwardly one is a huge slave of an unknown oppressor.

Man has immense power over his environment today, but man is himself controlled by his inner destructive centre he has very little knowledge about. Together, these two mean that man's tendency and ability to wreak havoc over his ecosystem is unlimited and unquestioned. Man has only one inner ruler—desire, the ever-sprawling desire to consume and experience more and more happiness. Happiness, that is experienced only to find that it evades all experience.

In this context, Vedanta—as the pure essence of spirituality—becomes more important today than it probably ever was. Vedanta asks the questions—Who is the inner one? What is his nature? What does he desire? Will fulfilment of his desires give him contentment?

As a response to the situations mankind today finds itself in, Acharya Prashant has taken upon the solemn project of bringing the essence of Vedanta to today's world. His calling is to bring the pure essence of Vedantic spirituality to all, and apply it to solve today's problems. The problems of today are borne out of man's ignorance towards himself, and therefore they can be solved only by sincere self-knowledge.

Acharya Prashant has approached the matter of bringing Vedanta to the public in a two-pronged way. One, he has spoken upon scores of Upanishads and the Gita and his comprehensive commentaries are available in the form of video courses and books (at solutions.acharyaprashant.org). Two, he addresses the daily mundane problems of people and demonstrates how to solve them in the light of Vedanta. His social media is dedicated to hosting tens of thousands of such open QnA sessions.

A Brief Biography

Prashant Tripathi was born in 1978, in Agra, India. Eldest of three siblings, his father was a bureaucrat and mother a homemaker. His childhood was spent mostly in the state of Uttar Pradesh.

Parents and teachers found in him a child who could often be quite mischievous, and then suddenly, deeply contemplative. Friends too recall him as having an unfathomable temperament, often not really sure whether he was joking or serious. A brilliant student, he consistently topped his class and received the highest commendations and prizes possible to a student. His mother fondly remembers how she was honoured several times as 'Mother Queen' for the academic performance of her child. Teachers would say that never before had they seen a student who was as brilliant in Science as in Humanities, as adept in Mathematics as in Languages, and as proficient in English as in Hindi. The then Governor of the state felicitated him in a public function for setting a new benchmark in the Board examinations, and for being an NTSE scholar.

The prodigal student was a voracious reader since he was five years of age. His father's extensive home library consisted of some of the world's best literature, including spiritual texts like the Upanishads. For long hours, the child would be tucked away in the most silent corners of the house, immersed in stuff that was meant to be understood only by men of advanced age and maturity. He would skip meals and sleep, lost in reading. Before he had turned ten, Prashant had read almost everything that was there in the father's collection and was asking for more. The first signs of the mystical appeared when he started composing poetry at the age of eleven. His poems were imbued in shades of the mysterious and were asking questions that most grown-ups could not grasp.

At the age of fifteen, after being in the city of Lucknow for many years, he found himself in Ghaziabad near Delhi, owing to his father's transferable job. The particular age and the change of city accelerated the process that had already taken deep roots. He took to staying up at night and, besides studying, would often be staring silently at the night sky. His poems grew in depth, a lot of them devoted to the night and the moon. Rather than academics, his attention started flowing more and more towards the mystical.

He nevertheless continued to do well academically and gained admission to the prestigious Indian Institute of Technology, Delhi. His years at IIT were full of exploration of the world, deep involvement in student politics, and shining as a debater and an actor in nationwide events and competitions. He was a most vibrant figure on the campus, a dependable student leader, and a soulful performer on the stage. He would consistently win debate and extempore speech competitions in which participants from across the country would compete and would also win prizes for directing and acting in meaningful plays. In one of the plays, he got the 'Best Actor Award' for a performance in which he did not utter a word and moved not a single step.

He had been sensing since long that there is something fundamentally amiss in the way most people perceive the world, the way our minds are conditioned to operate, and hence something distorted in the way the relationships between people are, the way the worldly institutions are designed, the way our society functions – basically the very way we live. He had started seeing that incomplete perception was at the root of human suffering. He was deeply disturbed by man's ignorance and cultivated inferiority, the evils of poverty, the evils of consumption, violence towards man, animals, and environment, and exploitation based on narrow ideology and self-interest. His entire being was raring to challenge the all-pervasive suffering, and as a young man, he guessed that the Indian Civil Services or the Management route might be an apt one to take.

He gained admission to the Indian Civil Services and the Indian Institute of Management (IIM), Ahmedabad in the same year. However, because the service allotted to him based on his rank was not IAS – the service that he had wanted, and because he was already seeing that the government is not the best place where revolutionary changes can be brought, he opted to go to IIM.

The two years at IIM were obviously rich in the academic content he absorbed. But he was not the one who would confine himself to slogging for grades and placements, as is the norm in these coveted institutions. He would regularly spend time in teaching kids at an NGO that operated in a slum close to Gandhi Ashram, and would also teach Mathematics to graduates to earn to spend at the NGO. Besides, his angst at human ignorance expressed itself through theatre. He took up plays like 'Khamosh, adalat jaari hai', 'Rhinoceros', 'Pagla Ghoda', and 'The Night of January 16th' and directed them, besides acting in them. At one point, he was directing two parallel plays. The plays were performed in the IIM auditorium to packed audiences from within and outside the city. In the profit-centered and self-interest driven atmosphere of the campus, he had found himself an outsider. These existentialist and rebellious plays helped him vent out his anguish, and also prepared him for the bigger stage ahead.

The next few years were spent, as he puts it, in the wilderness. He describes this period as one of particular sorrow, longing, and search. Looking for a piece of sanity in the corporate world, he kept switching jobs and industries. To gain composure, he would take time off and be away from the city and work. It was increasingly becoming clear to him that what he wanted to do, and what was crying out to be expressed through him, could not happen through any traditional route. His reading and resolve intensified, and he designed a leadership course for post-graduates and experienced professionals, based on wisdom and spiritual literature. The course was floated at some reputed institutions, and he would sometimes be teaching students elder than himself in age. The course met with success, and the way started becoming clearer to him.

At the age of twenty-eight, he bid goodbye to corporate life and founded Advait Life-Education for 'Creation of a new humanity through Intelligent Spirituality'. The method was to bring a deep transformation in human consciousness. The initial audience chosen was college students who were offered self-development courses. Wisdom from ancient literature was taken to students in form of simplified texts and engaging activities.

While the work of Advait was great, garnering appreciation from all and sundry, there were great challenges as well. The social and academic system has conditioned the students to study to just clear examinations and to have a degree to secure jobs. The self-development education, the education

of the Beyond, the life-education that Advait was attempting
to bring to the students was so new and so different from
everything that they had ever read or experienced that it
would often lead to indifference towards Advait's courses,
and sometimes even hostility from the system. Often even
the management body of the colleges and the parents of the
students would totally fail to grasp the utter importance and
immensity of what Advait was courageously trying to do.
However, amidst all these difficulties, Advait continued to do
well. The mission continued to expand and is touching and
transforming thousands of students.

Around the age of 30, Acharya Prashant started speaking
in his Samvaad, or clarity sessions. These were in the form
of open discussions on critical life-issues. Soon it started
becoming clear that these sessions were deeply meditative,
brought the mind to a strange peace, and had a miraculously
curative effect upon the psyche. Acharya Prashant's voice and
videos would be recorded and uploaded on the internet. And
soon a website too was developed to publish his writings and
the transcriptions of his talks.

Around the same time, he started organizing self-
awareness camps. He would take true seekers with him to the
Himalayas, in groups of around 30 each, for periods of around
a week. These camps turned out to be deeply transformational
events and the frequency of the camps increased. Hundreds of
camps have been organized so far providing immense clarity
and peace in relatively short spans of time.

Acharya Prashant's unique spiritual literature is at par with
the highest words that mankind has ever known. His genius is
founded on Vedanta. With his broad Vedantic foundation, he
is seen as the coming together of the various spiritual streams

of the past, and yet someone not confined by any tradition. He attacks the mind vigorously and simultaneously becalms it with love and compassion. There is a clarity that radiates from his presence and a soothing effect from his being. His style is forthright, clear, mystical and compassionate. The ego and the falseness of the mind do not find a place to hide in front of his innocent and simple questions. He plays with his audiences – taking them to the very depths of meditative silence, laughing, joking, attacking, explaining. On one hand, he appears as somebody very close and approachable, and on the other hand, it is obvious that the words coming through him are from somewhere beyond.

The 10,000+ videos and articles uploaded by him on the Internet, freely available to all, make the world's single biggest online repository of spiritual content of which more than 5 million minutes are watched daily. He has been regular speaker at IITs, IIMs, many other prestigious institutions, as well as platforms like TED. In print media, his articles get regularly published in national dailies. His discourses and interviews have been broadcasted via national TV channels too. Today, his movement has touched the lives of tens of millions of individuals. Through his direct contact with people, and through various internet-based channels, he continues to bring clarity to all.

PART I

HOW TO CHOOSE THE RIGHT ACTION?

What Is a Right Decision?

With IIT Kharagpur, 2020

What is the impact of your choices on your life? That is what you must look at. Are your choices making you more insecure, anxious, jealous, unsettled, restless? Then it would be dishonest to call these as right choices for you.

~

Questioner (Q): How to know whether a decision is right or wrong? What is right for one is wrong for the other. Nature has given everyone the right to choose. Who are we to criticize the decisions of others?

Acharya Prashant (AP): Right or wrong are not decided in the context of others. You're right, nobody has the right to label a person or a person's decision-making as right or wrong. However, it does not mean that there is nothing called a right decision or a wrong decision.

Understand it simply. What is it that we all fundamentally want?

We want peace.

We want relaxation.

We don't want to be tense.

We want contentment.

Ever seen anyone who enjoys being dissatisfied or diminished or hurt or angry? What is it that we all want? What is the common, universal need among humans? Peace and contentment. Nobody wants to be sad. We want a subtle joyful state of consciousness, and we all want that irrespective of the country we come from, irrespective of our age, our gender, our religion, our ethnicity. Nobody wants to be sad. Nobody wants to feel hurt.

So, if that is our core need, then you should know when to call a decision right and when to call one wrong.

If your decisions lead to peace, joy, and contentment for you, then they are right. Otherwise, they are wrong.

And this decision regarding a choice being right or wrong obviously is not coming from others; it is about your own inner self. What is the impact of your choices on your life? That is what you must look at. Are your choices making you more insecure, anxious, jealous, unsettled, restless? Then it would be dishonest to call these as right choices for you. And it is not in a relative sense; it is not as if one choice that is right for this person will be right for the other one also.

However, as we cautioned earlier, it doesn't mean that any choice is all right. There is definitely something called a right choice and there is definitely something called a wrong choice, and you have to be very careful because choices determine your life.

Next, you have mentioned that nature has given everyone the right to decide. Yes, that is true, and equally nature has given everyone the right to decide foolishly. Remember that it is just a right. A right is an option: you may choose to exercise it, or you may choose not to.

Unfortunately, most people do not choose to exercise this option wisely. What is the option all about? The option is: you could choose either from your heartful intelligence, or you could choose and decide from your conditioned self.

Choosing, deciding, or acting from your conditioned self is apparently easy because it hardly requires any effort. Therefore, most people allow their life, actions, thoughts, decisions, everything to come from their conditioned centres. It feels comfortable.

But then, the option to operate from the centre of heartful intelligence is available. That is what brings joy and contentment to you. That is what brings liberation to you. But that option is scarcely chosen because there is a price to pay, and few people want to pay that price. We are lazy and stingy. We don't want to work hard enough; we want to avoid exertion. We don't want to pay the price, so we don't go for the right option.

When you say that nature has given everyone the right to choose, remember that the right is often not exercised wisely.

It is upon you to make good use of the right, the power vested in you.

You could choose either from your heartful intelligence, or you could choose and decide from your conditioned self.

2

When to Think and When to Act

Advait Shivir, Bhopal, 2018

Thought is useful, but in matters of living, loving, and Truth, the utility of thought is limited.

~

Questioner (Q): I do not express my thoughts because I am socially restrained. I am afraid of being judged. Can I free myself only by deeds? Kindly throw some light on this.

Acharya Prashant (AP): Yes, of course. There is no more a final arbiter than action, deeds, life. What else is life, but a continuous flow of actions? One finally has to give oneself the liberty to do it. Talking as a precursor to doing is all right, acceptable, but talking as a substitute to doing is evil.

If you want to use talking or thinking or discussing as a preparatory method before leaping into action, it is okay. Sometimes, the beginner needs that. Sometimes, everybody needs to think a little before taking a leap. Sometimes, one needs to talk to herself, sometimes to others. All that is understandable. But if one becomes a professional thinker specializing in nothing but thought and deliberation, and therefore vacillation and inaction, then it is merely self-deception.

Also, I must warn you against the temptation to be fully sure at the level of thought. No absolute clarity is possible at the level of thought. Thought can bring you a certain level of clarity. However, it would be a relative level.

So, if you insist that unless you are totally clear with your thoughts you will not move, then you have ensured that you are never really going to move; then you will always have a reason to think a little more because thought by its very design can never be fully certain. An iota of doubt will always be residually present, and you can very well exploit that last iota to keep stretching the thought.

This is where faith is important. Faith is needed, so that you can act without being fully certain. At the level of thought, thought is still raising its habitual objections, but you say to thought, 'You might not be clear. I am clear.'

Have you ever found thought coming to a final conclusion? That which appears like concluded tonight reopens for discussion tomorrow morning because a final conclusion would mean the death of thought. So, why would mind ever lend itself to a conclusion? Thought would always leave a little scope for doubt to remain. And then, based on that doubt, that uncertainty, more thinking can be justified.

So, think if you must, but never expect thought to come to a solution. Thought is useful, but in matters of living, loving, and Truth, the utility of thought is limited. Do not try to overexploit thought. You will end up being exploited.

If you are saying that social restrictions, etc., are preventing you from enacting what you know, then you will have to weigh the security that you get from social conformity against the suffering that you get from this willing avoidance of your destiny.

What is bigger, your demand for security or your love for Truth? This answer will determine your life.

3

The Right Action Looks Strange, the Wrong One Looks Comfortable

Myth Demolition Tour, Rishikesh, 2016

If all seems to be going comfortably, chances are all is going wrong. If all seems to be nice, proper, sweet, hunky-dory, chances are everything is just patterned, known, conditioned.

~

Questioner (Q): Is there any action that is inherently bad? Where does the right action come from?

Acharya Prashant (AP): No, there is no action that is inherently bad. I repeat this with emphasis: *there is no action that is inherently bad.* The only bad action is a misplaced action.

At the right time and the right place, killing is wonderful. Coming is wonderful at the right time, and going is equally beautiful at the right time. Beginnings are lovely and so are the ends. There is nothing that is inherently avoidable.

But if you come at the wrong time, then coming is bad. Not only is killing bad at the wrong time, even giving birth at the wrong time is a crime. But if one is too body-identified, then one takes only killing as a crime because the body ends in the killing. When one is too body-identified, then one does not even talk of procreation as a crime.

Right time, right place, right action—only that is not a crime, only that is not inherently bad.

Where does the right action come from? You will never know. But you can surely know where the wrong action comes from. Where does the wrong action come from? Wrong action comes from one's own personal priorities, one's own likes and dislikes, one's own choices and preferences. Whatever comes from there is the wrong action. Whatever you decide and do for yourself, even with the best of intentions, is the improper action.

When you step back and let life function through you, that is the right action.

When you step back and let your personal priorities be subservient to something far bigger than yourself, that is the right action.

So, just do not give energy to the wrong action, to that which arises from the limited domain of your mind. If you do not give energy to that, if you do not side with that, then the right action will happen automatically.

The right action always looks strange. The wrong action always looks known because it is a repeated action, a conditioned action: we have seen it, done it, passed through it many times before. The right action is absolutely new, so new that you have no way of verifying it. And because you have no way of verifying it, it is easy to get afraid of it because you cannot go and ask somebody, 'Is this the right action?' Now, it is your action. You are entering into it for the first time. He has never had a taste of it, so if he is honest, he will say, 'I do not know.' Not only will he not know, but you too will also not know; even for you it is the first time. You cannot compare and check.

When such a thing happens with you—and I pray such a thing happens with all of us—feel delighted, do not let fear arrest you. It happens in those moments that fear comes to grip you. Just when you are about to fly free, *Maya* (illusion) tries its last recourse: it attacks with all the strength it has. Do not lose the battle at that moment. It is so sad when you lose a war that is so nearly won.

Forget the right action. Be cautious of the wrong action.

A hint: If all seems to be going comfortably, chances are all is going wrong. If all seems to be nice, proper, sweet, hunky-dory, chances are everything is just patterned, known, conditioned. If everybody is able to tell you, 'Oh, you have such a happy life, we are even envious of you,' if you tick all the right boxes in the social checklist, chances are everything is going wrong.

When things actually go right, only your heart knows that everything is going right. In the eyes of others, it is a total devastation: they feel like taking pity on you; they may ignore you; they may even become your enemies. For sure they know nothing of what is happening in your heart. Only your heart knows.

When that happens, thank God for that misfortune. It is the sweetest misfortune that you can have. It is a divine tragedy. It is the holiest blow that can strike you. Pray that it strikes you and shatters you totally, and then the right action happens.

Q: To take action in the world, one requires thought. Otherwise, you are just waiting for something to happen like a potato. How is it possible to act in the world if I do not know the right action?

AP: By seeing that you never really act even if you try to act.

You talked about waiting like a potato. Waiting is still an action; you are still an actor. So, even when you are waiting for that action to happen, you have not relinquished your claim of being the actor. As long as you have that claim, real action will not happen. You will just keep waiting.

Q: Who acts then? What creates action?
AP: We can never know that. We can never know where the right action comes from. Never! Don't even try that.

Q: Where does any action come from?
AP: Any action comes from our conditioned centre.

You can create a machine, and you can very well know where its actions are coming from: its actions are coming from the chip that you fed it, its actions are coming from its circuit, its actions are coming from its masters, its designers.

Similarly, in our case, most of the time our actions are just coming from what family, society, church, education, media, neighbours have taught us. It is enough to see that they are coming from there.

One's role is to just know the mind. In knowing the mind, the fakeness of the mind does not become too powerful. When you know that you are just acting as per how you have been taught to act, then you cannot be too serious about that acting. Then you create an empty space from where some other action can happen, and it happens on its own.

We have a great desire to know from where the right action happens. Do you see why we have that desire? What will you do if you come to know from where it happens? You will go there and sit on it, try to take control of it, do something with it, co-opt it, try to become its master, use it for your own interests. That is why it is such a relief that you can never know where the right action comes from. It is such a relief that God is unknowable. Had he been knowable, you would have gone to him and troubled him so much!

Just know where the false action comes from. It is easy to know that because it is in action all the time, visible all the time, operational all the time. Just know and honestly acknowledge that.

Forget about the real. The real is self-sufficient, it takes care of itself. You need not bother about it.

When you step back and let your personal priorities be subservient to something far bigger than yourself, that is the right action.

4

Spontaneous, or Carried Away?

With IIT Kharagpur, 2020

Spontaneity has to be earned. Otherwise, all that you will have is the spontaneity of machines or animals.

~

Questioner (Q): Why think so much about decisions? Shouldn't our decisions be spontaneous? I like to decide in a free flow.

Acharya Prashant (AP): The questioner is stressing on the spontaneity of decisions. It is a good thing. Your intention is good, but we have two flows within us: one is the flow of conditioning, the other is the flow of freedom.

In many ways, both these flows can appear similar or identical, and when you are in a flow, a stream, then movement is effortless; you get carried away. So, you have to be very careful about which stream you have chosen to be in: the conditioned stream or the free stream.

You are angry and you are saying a lot of things. In that moment, have you seen how the inner flow operates? In some sense, you are quite spontaneous at that moment, aren't you? But is there freedom in that spontaneity? Or is it just a kind of conditioned inner reflex?

You are standing in a barren and dark place, and somebody approaches from behind and taps your shoulder; you are shocked, and you respond with a jerk. You didn't have to think for this response. But is there freedom in this response? Or is this a totally conditioned response? The response was instantaneous, wasn't it?

That brings us to thought and time. Operating without thought and deciding without thought is a great objective to have, but you have to remember that there is a stream that flows above the zone of thought and a stream that flows below the zone of thought. When you decide using time, when you decide thoughtfully, then you are in the middle zone. But if your objective is to decide without using much thought, then you don't want to bring time into the picture.

Your objective, as you have mentioned in your question, is spontaneity. That can happen in one of two ways.

One, you become a totally conditioned machine, you start belonging to the stream below the zone of thought, and no time is needed there. It is like switching on an electric bulb or a fan: the moment you switch it on, the response from the machine is instantaneous. It is like bringing together two reactive chemicals: you bring them together, and the reaction is instantaneous.

There is no virtue in this kind of spontaneity because it is a totally conditioned spontaneity, and as human beings we are conditioned to a great extent. However, we have the freedom to choose whether we want to decide from the place and stream of conditioning, or whether we want to operate from the zone and stream of freedom. You have to be very careful.

Spontaneity by itself is not virtue. In fact, it is better to be thoughtful; it is better to take your time; it is better to reflect, meditate, contemplate. However, if your thought process is honest, then there comes a point when there is no need to think any further. When your inner faculty is trained to an extent that the need to think keeps continuously diminishing, a point comes when the time required to think is so small that you could claim that you are spontaneous. However, without training yourself fully, spontaneity is a thing to be warned of.

Spontaneity has to be earned. Otherwise, all that you will have is the spontaneity of machines or animals. They don't have to earn their spontaneity. A machine really did nothing to be spontaneous; it was designed that way. Similarly, animals are quite spontaneous in many ways; they don't really have to think or reflect or introspect. There is little worth in that kind of spontaneity. Therefore, it is much better to be thoughtful.

The faculty of thought is a very important power of the human mind; it must be utilized fully. However, that does not mean that one must keep thinking and thinking endlessly because, as you have mentioned in your question, a decision has to be made. And if a decision has to be made, you don't really have unending time. So, thought must have the objective of coming to a completion; thought must not become an end in itself. That is very important.

When you are thinking, you must continuously be aware of whether thought is just a tool to come to an ultimate end, or has it become a self-serving machine. Remember, the possibility of thought becoming a self-serving machine is significant. It happens with most people. We just keep thinking endlessly in some kind of a wasteful loop. You think about something and that induces fear or anxiety in you, and because of that, you are compelled to think more. And when you think more, it leads to more fear, and then this kind of a needless cycle continues. You find that you are going over the same thoughts again and again, going through the same kinds of imaginations and options and choices and logics again and again—and all of that is leading to nothing. When you find that you are caged in that kind of a circuit, then you should know that thought has become self-serving.

Thought has to be a useful tool, a servant. Thought must be used to come to something beyond thought because thought is movement. Thought implies lack of settlement; thought is like a journey: you have not yet come to the destination. The journey obviously cannot be the objective because in your heart you want to settle down and reach a destination, and that destination is a decision. You cannot feel relaxed unless the several options have been closed.

When thought proceeds, obviously it has several options to choose from, and all the mental activity is going on continuously. Thought feels empowered when there are options, but you feel discontented as long as there are options.

For thought to continue, there must be uncertainty.

For you to be relaxed, there must be certainty.

Therefore, in a position of uncertainty, in a situation of decision-making, use thought to come to certainty, to closure. Obviously, it should not be a forced closure, an artificial closure. It has to be an honest one. Thought has to be diligently applied so that a natural closure is attained. The intention has to be clear.

When you honestly apply thought this way, then the tendency of the mind to keep ruminating, to keep thinking, keeps diminishing over time. Slowly, you come to a stage where decision-making starts consuming progressively less and less time; you find that certain options don't appeal to you anymore, so you don't have to think about them. Since you don't have to think about them, the time that would have been spent in thinking about them and considering them and accepting or rejecting them is saved. Because that time is saved, the net time consumed by you in coming to the decision is small.

Do you see what is happening? You are approaching spontaneity. Then a point can come when you are truly spontaneous.

So, it is great to feel in control. It is great to not have to go through the time-consuming and laborious process of thought in decision-making. But that kind of luxury, I repeat, has to be earned. You have to earn your spontaneity. If you do not earn your spontaneity, I again repeat, your spontaneity is of the mechanical or animal type.

We want spontaneity that is associated with freedom. With complete freedom comes complete spontaneity. At the same time, there is no freedom in complete bondage, so things are instantaneous. A slave has no option to disobey: when the master calls or commands, he has to instantaneously obey. Looking from a distance, you could call this spontaneity. But is this the kind of spontaneity we want? Not really, right?

Have the spontaneity of a free person and not that of a slave.

Q: What bondage are we talking of? If we are indeed enslaved, who is our master?

AP: Our own innate, physical, primordial tendencies are our slave drivers. They command us. We talked about the machine and the animal. Let's take it forward from there.

Who commands the animal? The animal is commanded by its own physical constitution. The animal has no free will. The animal hardly has even any possibility of thought; the animal is not given that luxury or freedom. The animal does as its physical instincts command it to do. If the physical instincts say run, it runs. If the instincts say eat, it eats. If the instincts say sleep, it sleeps. It does not really think over anything. That is the first kind of bondage, the physical bondage, the very inner bondage.

Then there is the machine. Who commands it? The machine is commanded by the persons who designed it, who made it. The machine is commanded by a force outside of its physical self. In that sense, you could say that the machine is commanded by society. The machine has no free centre within itself. In fact, the machine does not even have its commanding master, its slave driver within itself. Where is the master of the machine situated? Somewhere else, somewhere outside of the machine. The master of the machine stands at a distance from the machine and holds the remote control.

In the case of the animal, its master is situated within its body. Though the animal is a slave, it is a slave to its own body. The machine is worse. The master of the machine is situated at a distance from the machine. Nevertheless, both the animal and the machine are enslaved.

This is the condition of every human being. We have two masters: one is our own body, second is the society outside of us. Our body rules us from within, society rules us from outside. We do not want either of these slaveries. We do not want to be ruled by our body, nor do we want to be ruled by society. That is freedom.

We talked of the conditioned flow and the free flow. The conditioned flow includes two currents: the physical, biological current, and the social current. The free flow includes none of this. In the free flow, there is just freedom, there is true spontaneity. That's the aim of living. That's the aim in all genuine decision-making.

Decide in a way that your decision is uninfluenced by your physical tendencies and your social conditioning. Only then would your decision bring joy and liberation to you.

5

How to Know What One Must Do

Advait Shivir, Mumbai, 2019

*Once you know what is Right, then surrender your
right to not choose the Right. If you continue to hold
that dangerous right, then inevitably at some point you
will use that right and un-choose the Right.*

~

Questioner (Q): You say that liberation is about being
disassociated from the things around us, to keep doing what
needs to be done without giving importance to results. But
generally, when we have to choose a career, we are advised to
figure out what our passion is. It is said the best work is based
on passion. I see a contradiction between these two. I do not
see how passion and disassociation from things can exist
together. Without any passion or attachment, how would I
know what I should be doing in my life?

Acharya Prashant (AP): How does one choose work? There
are broadly three ways.

First is when you choose work under external pressure or
in the flow of external situations, under the pressure of peers or
situations or market forces. It often involves happenstance. For
example, one happened to get placed in a particular industry in
the campus placement process. One just happens to get placed,
and one's career starts rolling on in that particular direction.
Soon that becomes the general direction of life.

The second way is that of passion. One says his work is based on his passion. This is just marginally a superior situation compared to the previous one because what we call as our inner urge or passion towards a particular work is something very conditioned.

It is difficult to be born in India and be passionate towards ice hockey. You will have very few kids saying that they want to make rugby or ice hockey their career, whereas so many kids are very passionate about cricket.

So, we know where passion comes from. It is not internal. Passion, too, comes from surroundings. It is a type of deeply internalized conditioning.

But passion is deceptively dangerous because it presents itself as something internal. Not only that but it also decorates itself as something of the heart.

The fellow will say, 'My heart beats for cricket.' You must ask him: Why doesn't your heart beat for ice hockey? Just because you have had no conditions favourable for ice hockey, you have not been conditioned towards ice hockey. You are conditioned towards cricket because there was cricket on the TV, there was cricket in the journals, on the radio, in the park in front of your house, or your elder brother put a cricket bat in your hand when you were just three years old. You were seeing all these things and they were having an influence on you. The result is: you didn't even get to know when you absorbed and internalized all these things. And you have started saying, 'Well, my heart beats for cricket.' Were you born in Brazil or Russia, would your heart still beat for cricket?

So, passion is as much an external thing as peer pressure.

Somebody chooses his work or livelihood going by market forces or peer pressure or family pressure, and then there is someone who says, 'I am choosing my passion for my livelihood.' These two are hardly different. Even if one is better than the other, the difference is marginal.

Compared to these two conditions, there is a distinct third possibility as well: a decision, an action, that comes from the centre of understanding. This third possibility deserves our attention.

You realize what is valuable, you realize what is life-affirmative, and you find it missing. You find that there is something that needs to be promoted, something that needs to be done, and then you do it. Not because you want to do it, but because you *must* do it. You don't do it because it is something quite attractive or remunerative; you do it because it *needs* to be done. There is no option. It is a call, it is sacred duty. You cannot avoid it. And only then is the work chosen by you really appropriate.

These are two words that you must be very careful about: 'want' and 'must'. 'I want to do this thing' versus 'I must do this thing'. These are dimensionally different statements.

All 'want' is conditioned. 'Must-ness' is an entirely different thing. 'This must be done. In front of this, it doesn't matter what I feel, how I think, what my ideals are, what my situations and conditions are. This *must* be done irrespective of everything.'

The one who starts living, abiding in this must-ness starts living at the pinnacle of life. It is a different zone of existence altogether: a point where you have just silently achieved all the spiritual goods.

Detachment? You have achieved.

Renunciation? You have achieved.

Witnessing? Yes, you are there.

Dispassion? Yes, you are there.

Commitment? Determination? Surrender? Yes, all of them become available to you, all the so-called spiritual goodies. They just come to you in a bunch as if they are all shadows of must-ness.

Where there is must-ness, there is the climate of spiritual benevolence.

This must-ness is classically called as Dharma: doing not what you desire to do, doing that which you must do.

And that is the only thing that makes all the difference in life. Are you doing something because you desire to do it or are you doing something because you must do it?

And remember, this must-ness is not a thing of duty or external pressure or moral responsibility; this must-ness does not come from those places. It is not about saying you must help your neighbour or you must be kind to people. No, not that kind of must-ness. We aren't talking moral science here. It is a very different must-ness. It comes from realization.

We said it proceeds from the core of understanding. Having really understood, a few things become totally unavoidable now. Once you know you are helpless, you must do what you must. You may even have a desire to roll back the reel and say, 'Well, I don't know at all, and because I do not know, I am free from the obligation of must-ness.' But you know and you cannot un-know what you know.

That is the thing about understanding. If you really understand, then you cannot roll back the process.

Once you really understand, then you don't own the understanding; the understanding owns you.

And once you are owned by understanding, obviously your own personal desires hold no value; now value belongs to the owner.

Q: How do I know this calling? When will I be able to recognize this?

AP: You will have to look at yourself and the world. If everything is perfect, then there need not be anything to do.

There is a stain on the wall and a fire in the kitchen. Both need to be taken care of, and we are being asked, 'Both need to be taken care of, so how do I decide which one comes first?' There is a stain on the wall and there is fire in the kitchen, everything is burning. Do you need to ask me which one holds a higher importance?

Q: What if there is fire in both the rooms?

AP: Then you figure out which room has the baby, or you figure out in which room you are trapped in or you figure out which room has more people or you figure out which room contains the gas cylinder. That is what is meant by observation. Observe the world and observe yourself, and you will know what is it that *must* be done. And then give up the right to un-choose what deserves to be chosen.

Once you know what is Right, then surrender your right to not choose the Right. If you continue to hold that dangerous right, then inevitably at some point you will use that right and un-choose the Right.

This is what is meant by surrender. Must-ness necessarily involves surrender.

Q: And will I choose to do it irrespective of whether I will be able to complete it or not?

AP: Yes, yes.

Q: Because it has to be done.

AP: Yes, it has to be done, and I may have a very clear idea that I will not succeed, but it needs to be done. It *must* be done. I have no option but to do it irrespective of the situations, irrespective of the conditions, and obviously irrespective of the outcome.

And it's not that I will blindly rush into doing it. I have my resources now; I know what needs to be done. I will marshal my resources in the most intelligent way possible. Not that I will blindly present myself for massacre, not that I will walk into a slaughterhouse. I have intellect. I have memory. I have capability. I can analyse. I can think. I can plan. All these are gifts available to me. This is my ammunition and I will use all of this towards that which must be done.

Q: There are a lot of things that must be done. The fire may be in this room or in the neighbour's house or in the Amazon forest. There are many levels to it. To what extent should we say that something must be done, and to what extent should we say that it doesn't matter to us?

AP: Take into account the criticality of the situation, and you know that your job is to do something about it. And that something is not just a token contribution; it has to be something very meaningful, as effective as you can make it. Weigh in on all these things and see how you must start.

You know, when you are asking that there are so many things and what is it that needs to be done, I am reminded of the time when Mahatma Gandhi returned from South Africa to India. He had been in South Africa at the centre of a civil movement for quite a while, almost more than two decades. In between, he kept coming to India to attend Congress sessions and to visit and other things, but there was not that much depth in those visits.

So, finally when he left South Africa for good and landed in India in the middle of the second decade of the last century, Gopal Krishna Gokhale told him, 'No public life for you for at least one year. Yes, you have been an outstanding leader in South Africa and you had victories and you have the capability to mobilize people and rally them behind you, but no public life in India for you for at least one year. Just abstain. Observe, watch, travel, know. First of all, read this country because there are just too many things at too many places. You cannot blindly rush into anything. At the same time, you cannot wait for long, Gandhi. You are already in your forties, and you are well equipped to do something. The kind of experience, the repository that you have cannot be allowed to go waste; it must be put in the service of the nation, but it cannot be immediately rushed. So, have some kind of a sabbatical for one year.'

Gandhiji considered Gokhale's teachings and followed his advice. He just kept studying. He realized there are so many things happening in this vast land from Burma till Afghanistan, from Tibet till Lanka. He started to get a handle on things, and then came the Champaran movement. It is not that he had consciously chosen to be in Champaran; that, too, was a kind of an accident. But when you are prepared, then very solemn accidents happen with you. Even accidentally the right things can happen to you—but only if you are prepared.

So, Gandhiji knew that there was something that needs to be done, but he didn't yet know what exactly that was.

So, he was reading, he was meeting people, he was travelling extensively, he was studying the Indian landscape. And then the accident happened. Somebody from a godforsaken village, a district in Bihar, came to him and kept shadowing him and said that such a thing is happening there and we need you to come and support us and defend our rights; the British masters are forcibly asking us to grow opium on fifteen per cent of our land, and that's exploitative.

If you are serious about the whole thing, what would you do? You would do what he did. You would read, you would meet, you would travel, you would observe, you would be alert all the time. You would want to find an opportunity. And it is far easier today, it is the information age. Even travelling is far easier today. At that time, to reach Champaran you had to travel on an elephant's back—that's how Gandhi reached there. Today, all these things are available; you can fly to the Amazon if you want to. And you don't even need to fly because all the information is available where you are. The videos are there; the perspectives are there.

So, your sincerity is judged by all the background work that you are doing—the effort. You cannot say you are very concerned with climate change and not know the scientific basis of all that is happening. You cannot just rush into some activity or the other; you cannot become a social media warrior or a placard soldier without putting in the effort to study the scientific fundamentals. Don't you want to study the science first? Don't you want to know what kind of actions are best suited if you want to fight this catastrophe? And if you do not know what action is best suited to fight it, how are you taking any action?

I am asking you, with no bias against tree plantation, how would you know that planting trees is the best way to counter this menace? Do you have the numbers? Without having the numbers, why do you want to offer a nominal service to the cause? Must you not first of all study, for example, the UN reports? And there are so many other organizations keeping a watch over the climate. Should you not find time to go through those reports and know what the whole thing is really about? Or do you just want to be a do-gooder? A self-deceptive feel-gooder? It is often fashionable to do all these things. It doesn't help.

Study! And then act with total commitment and determination.

If your action is founded on understanding, then your action becomes vigorous and irreversible. But if it is coming from some flimsy point, then such action has no momentum. It doesn't have longevity because it doesn't have sincerity.

6

Our Decisions Usually Come from the Animal Within

Advait Shivir, Pune, 2019

You are not the animal. You have the animal's body, but you have something that is not animalistic: you have a consciousness that is not content being an animal; you have a consciousness that seeks liberation.

~

Questioner (Q): If I do not take ownership of my actions, how can I make the right choices?

Acharya Prashant (AP): The choice has been made. The choice is to not take ownership. That is the most fundamental choice: whether or not to get associated.

The moment you say, 'I am not taking ownership of these actions,' the choice has been made. The choice is: 'I do not need to choose. If the action does not belong to my province, then all the choices will be made by the province to which it belongs. I stay away. I stay aloof. I don't need to make any further choices.'

By saying, 'I need to make choices,' the implication is: 'I love to be responsible.'

Q: The way I grew up, I was told that taking responsibility is a good thing.

AP: Taking responsibility is a great thing but take the *right* responsibility. Don't take responsibility for all kinds of

29

random and miscellaneous stuff. Your responsibility is your liberation. Your responsibility is not to meddle in the affairs of *Prakriti* (physical nature). In fact, the bondage is the meddling, the meddling is the bondage. Your responsibility is to keep away. Your responsibility is to find ways and courage and energy to keep away.

Q: If I am just letting the choices to be made, am I not allowing *Prakriti* to act?

AP: Yes, in her own province. And she knows the best that can be done in her province; you do not need to interfere. But that will require a bit of decentralization, devolution of power, and you do not like that, right? You want to hold on to the power. You are a control freak: 'I will decide, I am responsible.' You don't want to let her decide things that are essentially her stuff. She knows best. You do not know.

You say, 'I will take food at 8 a.m. and dinner at 8 p.m.' Who are you to decide? Let the stomach decide. 'But I follow a strict spiritual routine! At 4:30 a.m, sharp, I take my *nimbu pani* (lemon water).' No, no, no! Have you asked the body whether it even needs nimbu pani? And if it needs nimbu pani, it will attain it for itself.

When I say body, I also mean the brain. If the brain really needs something, the intellect will go in the direction of finding that thing. You don't need to interfere. You are redundant, useless. The entire system, the whole mechanism knows how to take care of its own interests, and its interests are purely material. Your interests are not material. Let the material take care of the material itself. It is a self-sufficient system. It will do what it wants to do, plus it has intellect as its servant.

Remember that intellect is also material. Remember that intellect, too, is a property of the brain. If the stomach needs water, the intellect will function in a way that will get it to water. Why do you need to meddle? But you like to control things!

Q: This is a bit confusing to me.

AP: Confusion is her province. Why are you taking ownership of confusion? Let the confused one be confused. You stay away. The intellect is confused? All right, that belongs to *Prakriti*. Let all the confusion happen there. You stay away.

Q: Survival of the fittest is also *Prakriti*. If I am competitive at work or if I think somebody is moving ahead of me or if I take unnecessary pressures, then this competitiveness is also *Prakriti*, right?

AP: Survival of fittest applies to animals. Their survival means physical survival. In your case, if there is physical survival without any peace to the consciousness, then it is worse than not surviving.

So, do not bring in Darwin to these matters. What he said applied only to the physical cell. The cell wants to survive, the DNA wants to replicate itself. That's not what your desire is. Remember who you are. You are not the cell containing the DNA. You are somebody else.

This DNA, this cell will take care of itself. If it wants to get involved in a race, in a competition to prove itself the fittest, to declare itself worthy of survival, it will do that. Your interests lie somewhere else. Your interests do not lie merely in the survival and continuation of bodies. Is that your interest? Your interests are different from that of the animal.

The animal's interest lies purely in survival of the species, continuation of the species, and betterment of the species. That's the animal perspective. The breed must keep getting better, the breed must keep multiplying, the DNA must proliferate. That's all the animal wants.

You are not the animal. You are, unfortunately, a little different. You have the animal's body, but you have something that is not animalistic: you have a consciousness that is not content being an animal; you have a consciousness that seeks liberation.

Remember who you are. Even if the body falls to pieces, you can gain liberation. That is a welcome thing.

Q: I will give an example. If I feel jealous about somebody . . .
AP: If the jealousy is enabling your liberation, be jealous. When you say you are feeling jealous, is the jealousy yours or does it belong to the *prakritik* domain? The test is: if it is yours, it has to be associated with liberation. Is jealousy enabling your liberation?

Q: No.
AP: Then it is not yours. It belongs to *Prakriti*. Why do you want to take ownership of jealousy? Jealousy is *prakritik*. Every animal knows jealousy. The newborn kid knows jealousy. Jealousy is ingrained, embedded in the cells.

You are not the cell. You are not the body. Remember who you are. You are the confined consciousness clamoring for liberation.

Q: My reaction to that should be what?
AP: Ask: Is this entire thing, the whole episode in any way associated with liberation? If not, then just stay away. If it

is associated with liberation, if it has a bearing upon your freedom, then act wholeheartedly. Otherwise, just stay away.

Q: So, I should not give it more importance.
AP: That's it, wonderful. That's the whole thing.

Q: I see that it is there, and ignore it.
AP: Exactly.

When I was in my teens, that was the one question I would repeatedly ask myself. 'What is important?' In some way, my entire journey began with that question. That question would not leave me. I would keep asking: what is important, and if there is stuff that is not important, why am I in it?

What is important? That which corresponds with your liberation, that alone is important. Everything else is just to be kept aside.

Q: Is seeking validation also a part of this *Prakriti*?
AP: See whether validation leads to survival of the species. Often it does. Animals, too, seek validation. Social consciousness is found very prominently in many, many animals, especially the more evolved species.

Validation is always social. You do not seek validation from the true self. You go out to seek validation from somebody else, and that is society. That social behaviour is very marked in most animals, especially primates. The more evolved the species, the more it tries to be socially acceptable. Its members do try that, and that leads to a continuation and proliferation of the species.

If the alpha male, for example, in a chimpanzee group is quite acceptable, then it is more likely that he will get the best females. That is a trick of *Prakriti* to produce the healthiest offspring possible. You cannot lead a group of gorillas, for example, without being socially acceptable to them.

A chimp has received validation and, therefore, he is the leader of the pack. What is that social validation ultimately leading to? Sex and healthy kids. That is all that *Prakriti* wants. Sex and healthy kids and more and more of that.

All these things that you find in corporate workplaces, boardrooms etc., they are things of the jungle. That is animalistic behaviour. That is jungle behaviour being replicated in sophisticated forms, in corporate places. It could even be parliaments. What you find happening there is essentially behaviour coming from the jungle, survival of the fittest. That will not help you. That will only help *Prakriti*. Remember that your goals and her goals are very, very different. That which helps her does not necessarily help you.

Therefore, the kind of yoga today that says, 'Keep the body healthy, and by keeping the body healthy, ultimately you will be enlightened,' is very false. And a lot of that is being promoted. They are saying that you just take care of the body, and that will take you to transcendence one day. That will not happen.

It does not matter what you do with the body; you will not gain liberation.

In fact, if you do a lot with the body, you will become more and more body conscious. Are all the fit people, the models, the athletes getting liberated? Are they? Do they even appear closer to liberation than the ordinary folk? No.

When you take so much care of the body, you become all the more body conscious. Day and night they are telling you, 'Do this with the body, do that with the body, eat at this time, sleep at this time, do this practice, that meditation, this *śuddhi* (purification), that *kriya* (practice),' and all that is related to the body. You are just doing stuff that will produce better and healthier kids. This is kid yoga. This is essentially going to produce more vital offspring, nothing else. It will not give liberation to anybody.

Therefore, there is also a lot of belief that physical health and spirituality are somehow interconnected. No, they are not. In fact, many among the ones who had a burning desire for freedom could not continue with their body for long. Let alone physical well-being, the physical existence itself is put at stake by the one who desires only freedom. Freedom is so big that you can easily do away with your body for its sake.

Recently, we celebrated Chandra Shekhar Azad's birthday at Advait BodhSthal. All of twenty-four was he, and his body was stronger and healthier than that of most yogis. It didn't take him much to just shoot himself. Today's cover page models would die to have a body like Chandra Shekhar Azad's, but while they keep fawning over their bodies and others' bodies, for Chandra Shekhar Azad the body was something that he could easily throw away: 'Here, the body. Ha! Nothing in front of freedom!' And it was not merely political freedom that he was targeting, you know that very well, right? They were well-read, well-educated people. They had a depth of understanding. What they wanted was total freedom, which meant freedom of the mind, which essentially is a spiritual thing to ask. You don't really want to do much with the body; you can just throw it away.

The body is to be used as a servant in the process of liberation. It cannot become the end itself. And even using it as a servant can be tricky because the body can be a very deceitful servant. When you say that you are trying to use the body, the fact might be that the body is using you instead; your perception regarding the body might be totally wrong.

So, the best thing is to leave the body to itself: 'You take care of your business, I will take care of my business. I don't even want you as a servant because you are not an honest servant.'

The body, even when you use it as a servant, is quite dishonest. You are using the body, for example, to come to listen to me. In between, you feel hungry and you sit down in a restaurant. What has happened? You are thinking that you are using the body to come to me, and you find that the body has used you to go to a restaurant instead. The body is a very tricky servant, to be used with care and caution.

Just because certain things are happening in very respectable companies—the word 'respect' itself is so dirty, is it not? Do not think that those things are sophisticated. Most of what you see happening around yourself, even in the most polished environments, is just stuff of the jungle, stuff of the street—the lion chasing the deer, jackals and hyenas clamoring for the leftovers, the dog chasing the bitch, stuff of that dimension. That is what you find happening in the corporations and even in the parliaments, even in the temples, everywhere. No need to give it too much respect. No need to be concerned too much with it.

Do you feel very, very concerned, do you take it as an event of cardinal importance when you find a stray bull poaching upon a vendor's stuff? Is it something that you would call earth-shaking, momentous, highly significant? It's just one of those things. The bull is there, and the vendor's cart is carrying those vegetables, and the bull has tried to satiate itself.

What you call a hostile takeover in corporate jargon, is it not the same thing as the bull trying to make its way to the vegetables? But there you say, 'You know, it has to do with company law. It's a hostile takeover. It's a thing of the well-read ones! You need to have an MBA to understand what is going on.'

You don't need an MBA. It's the bull and the vegetable! And in sum total, a lot of bullshit.

Our problem is of values. We have attached too much value to stuff that is inherently despicable. Stuff that deserves our contempt has commanded our adulation instead. You do not sometimes merely need to ignore some things, you actually need to be full of active contempt towards those things. It is only when the contempt becomes very deep that it turns into disdain, and then you can ignore.

If you are very respectful towards something, first of all learn to be actively disrespectful. That will allow you to break away; that will allow you to openly declare your freedom. Only later can you say, 'No, I don't even insult or humiliate those things; I just brush them aside.'

Usually, what we call 'brushing aside' is just our inability to take on the monster in the face squarely. Because we do not have the guts to take it on, we pretend that we are brushing it aside. We say, 'Oh no, I do not want to lock horns with that fellow. He is such a dirty fellow. I don't want to get tangled with him!' You don't *dare* to get tangled with him.

So, first of all, learn to dare. First of all, learn to be disrespectful. And when you know that you are so strong that your victory is guaranteed, then you can say, 'Who wants to fight a loser? Now I can just ignore him.' When you are the underdog, how do you say, 'I am giving the other one a walkover'? When you know he is silly, when you know he is so meek and weak, then you can say, 'I do not want to fight with him.'

The fact is that right now you are the underdog, and if you are the underdog, then you need to show some guts, some heart, and fight. When you become the champion, when you have the crown, when you sit on the throne, it is then that it behooves you to say, 'I ignore!'

Forgiveness and aloofness and detachment are not for the weak ones. If you know you are weak and you say, 'I am full of forgiveness, I stay detached,' then you are just trying to create a cover-up.

You are not the cell. You are not the body. Remember who you are. You are the confined consciousness clamoring for liberation.

7

The Only Action That Helps You Is That Which Helps Others

Course in Realization, BodhSthal, 2019

Love—That's your medicine. If your own suffering does not move you, then look at others' suffering.

~

Questioner (Q): My question is about suffering. With your guidance, I have to come to see that my life is nothing but a big lump of suffering. It includes the whole swing of pain and pleasure, attachment and aversion, and my role in them as the 'I'. Even so, I still feel that there is the impenetrable armour of numbness towards myself. There is no authenticity in this realization of suffering. There is no right action. It feels very dry. I keep listening to you, and sometimes your words penetrate through that armour. But still, again and again, I choose to stay in the dirt. The situation seems hopeless but not hopeless in the sense of surrender, but rather in the sense of becoming cynical.

How can I truly see anything when the instrument of seeing itself seems to be very polluted?

Acharya Prashant (AP): Love—where is love in all this? That's your medicine. Generally, that's the panacea. If your own suffering does not move you, then look at others' suffering.

You come from a country (the questioner is from Finland) where suffering is at least not obvious. Economic and technological development is a great veil; it hides so much. That's probably the reason why most of the saints happened to be in parts of the world where suffering was rampant, where suffering was an unavoidable fact, where suffering was something that you could see right on the streets.

It sometimes so happens that men of compassion become victims of their self-neglect. There are people who become victims of self-aggrandizing or self-centredness; equally, there are people who become victims of self-neglect. They just do not have the faculty to care too much about themselves. Therefore, if they are to go into their own suffering, if they try to feel motivated by their own suffering, if they are to try for liberation by using their own suffering as the reason, then they would fail because they just do not have the faculty to bother too much about themselves. If it is about themselves, they ignore it. It happens.

This, too, is ego. Just as self-centredness is ego, self-neglect is ego as well. It is a beautiful version of ego, probably one of its better versions. Nevertheless, it is still ego. And if it is ego, it avoids the Truth.

All this that you have mentioned is not working for you, nor is it probably going to work for you in the future. However, love would work for you. If it is not your own suffering that you bother about, look at others. But then, in that part of the world, the suffering of others is not so obvious, so you will have to find a way. You will have to go deeper into somebody's life. You will actually have to look for areas where people are willing to admit their suffering.

And why does it need to be about people, human beings? You very well know that human beings do not represent even 0.1 per cent of all beings on this planet. And we are not talking of the universe; we are not even talking of this galaxy; we are not even talking of this solar system—we are talking of this tiny planet! Why don't you work for living beings? There is ample suffering, I assure you. Your own little suffering can be alleviated only by partaking in the liberation of others.

If you see that you do not want to help yourself much, it is both bad news and good news. Your processes and your efforts are failing you, so don't try. Let them fail fully. Your system tells you, 'No, I am not interested in getting rid of my personal suffering,' so you must tell your system, 'All right, if you do not want to get rid of suffering, so be it. I am now going to turn even more unresponsive to you.'

Let the suffering be there. Pick up a great mission and proceed with it. Don't bother about whether or not you have any personal suffering. Maybe that's the medicine that your suffering has been asking for. It wants to be forgotten. It wants you to rise above your personal suffering. It wants you to help others.

Do you see how self-neglect and self-centredness go together? We said both are ego. We said one looks better than the other, but both are ego.

In this entire text that you have sent me, you have mentioned how you do not feel motivated to drop your armour. You have said, 'I choose to stay in the dirt.' You are saying, 'My instrument of seeing myself is very polluted.' You have said, 'I feel I have an impenetrable armour of numbness towards myself.'

Two things are very obvious from your description. One, you are not able to do much to help yourself; two—and this is where the problem lies—you are talking only of yourself. Where are the others? Your description itself suggests the prescription, and that's the advantage with honest descriptions. Very soon they turn into prescriptions.

So, my prescription is: If the 'I' refuses to get sorted, why don't you just ignore it? Why chase it stubbornly? Appears foolish, no?

How aesthetic does it look when a man is chasing his chicken, and the chicken is running all around refusing to be caught? And the man is distraught! Have you ever tried to run behind a hen or a cock or a chicken? How aesthetic and beautiful is the sight? And I am not talking of kids running behind these little birds; I am talking of grown-ups with all their spiritual sincerity—chasing chickens. That's how it looks when a man says, 'I am chasing the last rudiments of my ego, but I am unable to catch them!'

Ignore it, ignore it. That's the way. Ignore it and move into something bigger, vaster. A little bit of suffering is still there? Let it be there. I suffer so much, why must you not suffer? Who are you to not suffer? Why were you born? What if I start caring for my suffering? Not that I do not care for my suffering, but I do not let the chicken make me lose my weight. It does what it does. I just keep looking at it from the corner of my eye. I do what I do.

This concept of 'individual liberation' is a great myth. I have repeated it innumerable times. It won't happen this way. It cannot happen.

I am just entertaining you when I say that you are a man of compassion who is a victim of his self-neglect. Let me return to my unpolished and uncivilized self!

You are just a victim of good old ego, which is trying to somehow make its way out of a burning ten-storey building and yelling, 'I am stuck here! I am stuck here! How do I now move? Can't see the stairs! Can't see the firefighters! Where is the fire engine?' And all that it is talking about is 'I'. 'How do *I* get out of this burning building?'

There are others. Where are the others? At least for *you* there are others. Or do you live in perfect non-duality?

There are others. And if there are others, help them. For your own sake, help them. Just be wisely selfish and help them.

8

Forget Winning,
First Choose the Right Battle

Advait Shivir, BodhSthal, 2017

*Defeat is hardly ever to be measured in terms of the
events that happen outside of you. Defeat hurts exactly
because defeat happens inside of you.*

~

Questioner (Q): Why do we remain trapped in defeat? We
continue with our irregularities knowing fully well that we are
not doing justice to ourselves. At times, there is a strong feeling
to do better, but this feeling or commitment does not last.

Acharya Prashant (AP): In the right battle, there can be no
wrong result. Defeat is possible only when one is fighting
the wrong battle. If you find yourself defeated, and defeated
regularly, just know that you have picked up a battle that you
should never have been fighting in the first place.

Defeat is hardly ever to be measured in terms of the events
that happen outside of you.

Defeat hurts exactly because defeat happens inside of you.

How is it possible for any movement outside of you to
hurt you? That is the reason why Saint Kabir had to say,
'*Mann ke haare haar hai, mann ke jeete jeet* (You lose if the
battle is lost in the mind).' Mind is shaken up, impacted, and
hurt by an external happening—this is what we call as defeat.
Did this defeat happen when a particular event took place? Is

44

this defeat a result of an action? No, every defeat is a defeat right since the inception of the action.

If you are fighting a battle, if you are involved in something, and somewhere along the way that thing, the process, the result of an action starts hurting you, it only means that you started from a position of inadequacy and incompleteness in the very first place. You start from a point of incompleteness and you fight, you strive to somehow get over the incompleteness.

The beginning itself is wrong. The end will follow the beginning.

When you have begun wrongly, the process cannot correct the beginning.

You are proceeding with the wrong idea. You are proceeding with an assumption. You are driving from the wrong place with the wrong map. Now, even if the process of driving is immaculate, it would not help.

You might be a great driver, but if you do not know where you are coming from and where you are going to, then your driving skills will only take you to the wrong place faster.

What has begun wrongly cannot be corrected by the finesse involved in the process. Since it has begun wrongly, it will lead to more despair. We are often more concerned about winning and losing than simply knowing whether we are fighting the right battle. If you are fighting the wrong battle and you win, is it not worse than losing?

What is a wrong battle? A wrong battle is one that is needless, just as incompleteness is needless. It is unnecessarily there, it need not be there, it has no utility, it really has no existence. Even if it is not there, there would be peace. In fact, there would be peace *only* if it is not there.

We often fight battles that are absolutely needless. Of what use is winning such a battle? If you win such a battle, you may in fact continue along your ways, consoling yourself with the victory. Incompleteness is the wrong place to begin a battle. One suffers from an inferiority complex and because of that one wants to conquer the world. One may want to enroll in an institution. One may want to earn riches. One may want to have money or a big house. One wants all that because firstly one felt bad about their present condition.

One feels bad about his condition only when he strongly identifies with his condition.

You might be carrying a dead, stinking rat in your hand. It does not make you feel bad about yourself because you have not identified with it; you know you are just holding it and you can drop it at any moment. But if you mistakenly forget that it is possible to drop the rat and the rat becomes a part of your identity, personality, then you will be in trouble: you will keep holding the rat because it is now a part of your being. That's what you have told yourself.

Now, you keep holding the rat and you make efforts to get rid of all that which comes with being associated with the dead rat. Your efforts are fundamentally misplaced. You should have not proceeded with the efforts at all. In fact, by proceeding with your efforts, you are only assuring yourself that your assumption about yourself had some substance.

You are trying so hard to cleanse yourself, to wash your face; you are scrubbing yourself all over the body. At this moment, if someone comes and tells you that you are already neat and clean, you would feel like an idiot. It is now necessary to convince yourself that there is something terribly filthy about you. That is how your effort would be justified.

Look at this stupid and dangerous loop. Some people take a bath because they are feeling dirty; others convince themselves that they are dirty because they are compulsive bath takers. 'Because it is a habit with me to take a bath, because I have made it mandatory to keep rubbing myself and polishing myself every few hours, I convince myself that I am indeed filthy and stinking.' That is how most wrong battles are fought: because you must fight, because fighting and conflict have become a necessity in one's mind.

One justifies oneself by saying that the war is needed. The mind is like a weapons factory: to continue with its output, it needs wars. Why else are you producing all the fighter jets and cannons and aircraft carriers? There must be war. So, there are weapons that are produced to fight wars, and there are wars that are fought because too many weapons have been produced. Now, something has to be done with those weapons, otherwise, how do you justify the factory?

Unfortunately, most of our wars are production-led. Because the mind is habituated to fighting, it picks up some war or the other. The entire life has been built around wrong assumptions, and all wrong assumptions are, in some sense, cunning: they are there to hide something else. One might be in the business of weapons just because one is too lazy to learn something else. You won't accept that you are too lazy to move and learn, you would rather keep asserting that war is necessary.

If your self-image is that of a warrior—'Who am I? Someone who conquers enemies'—then you need wars. The enemy might not necessarily be a person; the enemy might be a situation. Any challenge is tantamount to a war. Now, if you must uphold your image, you must seek war, build wars rather.

Defeat is not the end of the war. Mostly, defeat lies in the beginning of war.

A needless war, the moment it begins, the point from where it begins, is already a defeat. Now it does not matter whether after a time the formal result, the apparent result looks like a victory or a defeat. We are great losers in life not because we meet with regular defeats but because we are fighting the wrong battles. Most of our effort, our conflict, our strife, is simply unnecessary. We need not have entered it.

Man has only two options: Either see who you are and what you have and delight in it, simply feel grateful, or do not see who you are and what you have, and keep wallowing in self-pity and incompleteness, and, therefore, keep picking unnecessary battles.

The more you pick unnecessary battles, the more you will feel defeated.

The more defeated you feel, the more will be the urge to fight another unnecessary battle.

It is a downward spiral. Once caught you remain caught.

The question says, 'Why are we regularly in the lapse of defeat?' Now you know. The question says, 'Even if I become determined, the feeling or the commitment does not last.' It is because the determination is for the wrong cause. You are determined to win but you are not determined to abandon the war. You are determined to reach the wrong place at the right time. Would that help?

You are going to attend a party, and you are on the wrong road. You are proceeding in the opposite direction, and you are hurrying. Because you think you have only twenty minutes and twenty miles to cover, you rush, and in twenty minutes you indeed do cover twenty miles—but where have you reached? The wrong place. Your determination did not really help you. In fact, your determination only hurried your downfall.

Willpower, commitment, determination, they are of so little use because they are extremely superficial.

One can be a very committed person and yet have a very petty mind because one is needlessly committed—committed to the wrong thing from the wrong centre.

There are autocrats and dictators, and they have armies of committed soldiers. Commitment in itself is not at all of any value. Value belongs to the place the commitment is coming from, and therefore, the place the commitment is going to.

It is the same with discipline. One can be a very disciplined idiot. Discipline by itself is, again, of no value. One could be going to the wrong workplace every day at the right time. Of what use is such discipline?

One might be very diligent with the wrong tasks. Of what value is diligence? One might be very efficient in the most nonsensical of procedures. Of what value is efficiency?

Efficiency or discipline or determination or commitment make sense only when the fundamental has been taken care of. After you are devoted to the right thing from the right centre, then comes the question of discipline, of remaining committed, of hard work, diligence, etc.

One has to know the centre one is operating from, otherwise, the action can be very deceptive. You are digging the earth. Now, you might be digging a grave, or you might be digging the foundation of your palace. Who knows? And you are very diligent and very efficient. But what really are you digging?

Willpower, commitment, determination, they are of so little use because they are extremely superficial. One can be a very committed person and yet have a very petty mind because one is needlessly committed—committed to the wrong thing from the wrong centre.

9

Sometimes the Right
Action Appears Like Inaction

Advait Shivir, BodhSthal, 2017

*It's not a lack of action that bothers you; it's lack of
prescribed action that bothers you, it's lack of action
that 'conforms' which bothers you.*

~

Questioner (Q): Why am l not able to take action? Why do I
remain so confused with respect to the fact that I have to do
something? I am trying to pretend that l am immersing myself
in something l like, but my mind is still confused.

Acharya Prashant (AP): There is no obligation to act.

The world that we live in places a compulsion upon us:
'Be an actor, be an achiever, go ahead, do something!'

It is not mandatory.

Look at the mango tree, the fruit is probably the action
of the tree. The tree has done something. For years, many
years, there is no action, no visible action, and then one year
you find that there is the fruit—little flowers, buds, and then
the fruit. The tree does not act under any compulsion to act.
Something keeps ripening within and ultimately that ripeness
shows in the luscious mango. The ripeness of the mango is the
ripeness of the tree.

You are saying you are not able to act. Aren't you acting
every day? Why do you find that action insufficient? It is not

a lack of action that bothers you; it is the lack of prescribed action that bothers you, it is the lack of action that 'conforms' which bothers you.

You want action that conforms to the wishes of others or your own. You want action that is as per established patterns and you are willing to call only that as genuine action. So, if you are reading something, you do not admit that as legitimate action, or if you are in meditation, or if you are just watching a mountain, you do not call all that as action.

What do you call an action? Achieving something, earning something, rising in career, building a house, conquering a city. Now, all of these, according to you, are gainful, meaningful actions. And the mango tree, you would say, is not acting at all.

Cast away the images that you have, stop having role models, stop believing in fairy tales. Maybe you are too much under the influence of movies—that too action movies.

Just live!

Just live, action is inevitable.

You cannot stop action even if you want to. It is not within your control.

Action will keep happening; you don't have to push it, you don't have to push at it.

If you understand what life is and who you are, then you will also understand the right action and when it is needed.

Don't impose upon yourself a code of model action.

Remain attentive!

Keep asking, 'What is all this?'

And then you will find that good, proper, peaceful action will happen on its own. If that action requires planning, you would find that you have an inner urge to plan. If that action requires accumulation of resources, you will find that you are being implored to gather resources. All would start happening. But let all of that be rooted in your understanding; don't hanker after action.

The world is suffering a lot because there are just too many people acting.

We need many more people who refuse to act, who are not so obsessed with acting.

Look at the problems of the world today. Aren't they all arising from unnecessary and misplaced action? So many of mankind's problems would be solved if we just cut down on our actions; not increase them or improve them but simply cease, simply come to a full stop.

Don't rush, don't be impatient.

You aren't here to act; you are just here.

You aren't here to do something; you are just here.

Most of us live life as if we are compensating for a sin, as if we have to pay a price for living, as if we must make up for something lost. We live life as if we are exonerating ourselves of some fundamental guilt. We live life as if we have to earn a certificate and display it to someone.

The world is suffering a lot because there are just too many people acting. We need many more people who refuse to act, who are not so obsessed with acting.

PART II

WILL THE RIGHT ACTION
GIVE THE RIGHT RESULT?

10

If You Are Unable to be Fully Involved in Your Task

With NIT Jamshedpur, 2020

If the choice is coming rightly, then what you are doing actually becomes a love affair, then you just cannot drop it easily. You become helpless in the matter.

~

Questioner (Q): You always emphasize on total involvement in any task one takes up, but life is a constant flux. One gets distracted. How to remain fully involved in our tasks?

Acharya Prashant (AP): The task has to be special and overwhelming enough. You cannot say that you want to remain fully immersed in just any task amid all the changes, the flux, the ups and downs of life. That won't happen. You must have something utterly important at hand. It must be something so overpowering that it demands your entire energy, the weight of your total self. Only then will you be able to remain dedicated irrespective of all the distractions and movements around you.

So, the question has to be reworded. You have to be very clear about what your task should be.

It is a very common fallacy. People often say, 'I want to remain committed to my work, my tasks, my profession, my studies, my resolutions. I want to stick to all these things, but

I lose track, I start feeling distracted,' and then their entire curiosity is about how to not get distracted. They would never ask: what is it that you do not want to get distracted for? What is it that you have picked up? What is it that you want to stick to? Why do you want to avoid distractions?

Look at the assumption in your question. What you are saying is: 'There is something that I have picked up, I must stick to it; therefore, I must not get distracted.'

I am asking you a more fundamental question: Why must you stick to what you have picked up? What is the need? Is your task important enough, meaningful enough, right enough? If it indeed is, then no distraction will be able to budge you, let alone uproot you.

Mostly, it is not that the distractions are too powerful; it is just that the task that we take up is so underwhelming, so little that our association with it is very feeble, very powerless. This powerless association is then defeated by even a simple kind of distraction.

Right now, as I speak to you and look out of the window, there is a strong wind blowing. Strong and deep-rooted trees don't have to worry. They have associated themselves so deeply with their foundation that it does not matter to them how strong the wind is. It does not matter to them that some large animals occasionally come and start violently rubbing against their trunk. The trees stand where they are. The trees do not say that the world is too full of distracting and uprooting forces.

Why don't we want to look at what we are doing? Why do we just talk of the distractions and disturbances? We don't want to look at what we are doing because the task that we have picked up is a function of our ego. And if you carefully investigate the task you have picked up, it would very quickly become an investigation into the very nature of your life, and you would be forced to change your life. That hurts. That hurts in the psychological sense and demands a lot of effort, so we do not want to look at our choice of work and the choosing agency that executes that choice. That we do not bother much about. But we do need to bother about that.

In fact, one must be distracted. Why should you remain focused on an unworthy task? Sometimes, it is better to see that the task that you have picked up has come to you either in ignorance or just accidentally; you really have no heartfelt relationship with it. Your weak association is exposed the moment there is something else trying to claim your attention. You find that you are attracted towards that other thing very easily; you just slip away. And if you just slip away, it merely means that your fundamental relationship with your task is very weak. It is weak because the choice of action has come from an unconscious state of the actor; you really have not decided what to do very consciously or honestly.

If the choice is coming rightly, then what you are doing actually becomes a love affair, then you just cannot drop it easily. You become helpless in the matter. A situation may come where you may actually want to leave the work you are doing, but the work itself will be so compelling that it won't allow you to go away. It is a diametrically opposite situation.

You are saying, 'I want to be with my work, but worldly distractions come and carry me away.'

If you really know what you are doing, if you really see the importance of the work with respect to your life, then even if you find that you want to leave your work, a deeper point within you does not allow you to go away.

So, don't talk too much about the distractions. Talk about yourself and the choice of your work. You must see what your deep needs are, and your work has to correspond to those needs. That is anyway the sole motive of all right work. Otherwise, why should one work at all?

Work has to be purposeful. The sole purpose of work is to bring contentment and completeness to the incomplete psyche within. You have to figure out what it is that your mind lacks, and your work has to be chosen so that it brings the required fulfillment and completeness to your mind. Then your mind will never feel alienated or bored from your work because now the mind can see and experience that the work is indeed very beneficial.

Remember, the work is beneficial, not the result of the work. Just the process of working itself is so beneficial. Who is going to wait for the salary cheque or the results of the examination? The joy from the work is instantaneous, you are not working to get some possible benefit in the future. Right in the middle of action, you are deriving joy from the action. Where is the possibility of getting disturbed or deviated now? Who can now take you away?

That is why I said it is a love affair. And it is a hearty love affair that cannot be so easily snapped.

The sole purpose of work is to bring contentment and completeness to the incomplete psyche within. You have to figure out what it is that your mind lacks, and your work has to be chosen so that it brings the required fulfillment and completeness to your mind.

11

In Detachment, Right and Vigorous Action Happens

Course in Realization, BodhSthal, 2018

Detachment is not about breaking relationships.
Detachment is about setting the relationships right.

~

Questioner (Q): How do I practice detachment with my children when it has always been a bond of attachment? How to let go and remain detached even when I know that the children are making wrong choices?

Acharya Prashant (AP): Detachment does not mean passivity. Detachment merely means that now you have your hands free to take the right action. If your hands are tied to the hands of another person, how will you help him? Tell me. If your hands are tied to my hands, how much can you do for me? It will be difficult for you to even serve me some medicine; it will be difficult for you to even cook some food for me.

When you are detached from someone, you gain the freedom to actively help that person. Detachment is not about passive observation, kindly get over that concept. Detachment does not mean that now you have nothing to do with the person you are detached from. Detachment rather means that now your love is free to act rightly. In attachment, how will you act rightly? Very difficult.

Love and right action go together. Therefore, there is no love in attachment. Detachment and love go together. And this must be sounding a bit strange to you because usually the love image is two people hugging each other, and the detachment image is a man looking passively, nonchalantly, almost in a forlorn way, at the ways of the world.

So, the house is on fire, and your detachment story says, 'The detached one just kept watching as the house burned.' No, detachment does not mean that the detached one will keep watching as the house burns. Detachment means that when the house burns, you still stay right at your centre; you do not allow your feelings, instincts, or attachment to cloud your wisdom, and, therefore, you remain capable enough to act vigorously, rightly, helpfully.

Detachment is not about breaking relationships. Detachment is about setting the relationships right.

Many householders find the word 'detachment' very scary. Equally, they find the word 'attachment' quite attractive. You tell someone, 'I am feeling quite attached to you,' and that someone will find it difficult to hide a smile—it is so very flattering! 'You know, these days I am feeling a bit attached to you,' whereas this is the scariest statement you can hear from anybody. When somebody tells you he is feeling attached to you, run away. Tell him to turn around and count till twenty, and say, 'When you reach twenty, I will demonstrate how attached I too am.' Twenty should be enough for you to fly ten miles away.

Attachment means the other fellow is now going to act almost as a parasite, a bloodsucker or a possessor. And there is nobody who wants to possess you as much as a parasite. A parasite has a deep need to possess its host, its prey.

Detachment and love go together. In fact, you cannot have love without detachment. If you find that you have love accompanied by attachment, then your love is very polluted.

Love is when you do not care about your self-interest and your objective is the welfare of the other. Attachment is when you cling to the other for your own sake. Now, can love and attachment go together?

So, stay detached, stay loving, and act fully, act rightly.

12

How to Balance Detachment and Action?

Course in Realization, BodhSthal, 2017

Great action cannot happen in attachment. One is attached always to the little, and only little action is required to acquire the little, so how will attachment lead to great action?

~

Questioner (Q): Ashtavakra Gita has had a profound impact on me. I feel deeply peaceful and blissful, and that helps me do my work better. However, I also feel detached from my work, which might affect how much effort I put into it. How should one balance detachment and action?

Acharya Prashant (AP): They are one. It is not an either/or thing.

First of all, you tell me, what is the quality of your action when you are not detached? Commonly you think that when you are not detached, then you can work with motive, with energy. To an extent, you are probably right. Attachment does bring out a certain quantum of energy. Attachment compels you to act and provides you with motive—but only to certain action.

Great action cannot happen in attachment. One is attached always to the little, and only little action is required to acquire the little, so how will attachment lead to great action?

Attachment is surely an agent of movement and action. But, at the same time, attachment guarantees that your action will be confined, limited, and mediocre. You will act, but you will act in a petty way. Your action will never have immensity.

But we try to look at the so-called positive side: we say attachment at least ensured that we acted, fear at least ensured that we moved. If you remove attachment, if you remove fear, then we are afraid that we will not act and move at all. That is not true. When you are not attached, then you will not move the way you *used* to move. But is that way of movement, that way in which you used to move, the only possible way of moving?

You know one quality of movement: movement caused by fear and greed. 'I am afraid of something, I run away from it. I want something, I run towards it.' These are the only two types of movement we usually know of. Does that mean that these are the only two qualities of movement possible? No. There is another quality possible.

When an Ashtavakra touches you, when detachment purifies you, it is not as if you stop moving; you merely stop moving in the way you used to move. A new quality of movement descends upon you, and I assure you, this quality has more energy, greater power, more sustainability.

It does not get defeated easily.

It does not get exhausted.

It fights but without effort.

It is not frustrated because it does not have high hopes.

It keeps continuously working because it is not expecting results from the work, and because this quality of movement is not dependent on external situations, it has a certain sustainability.

It does not show abrupt spikes and falls.

It does not exhibit itself greatly.

It is powerful but passive.

It is highly communicative but silent.

It does great things without making a show of it.

Your question is similar to the question of another man. You know what the question of that other man was? He said, 'I had a 500cc, old, rusted, decaying, failing car somehow kept on the road with a lot of effort and maintenance. I used to manage to go till the marketplace using this car. The marketplace is 10 kilometres away from my home, and this car would carry me till there. Now, with some good luck, I have a bigger 2000cc car, a new one with fine movement and fine controls and very little noise and far less smoke. Those who sold this car to me told me that this car is meant for great jobs: "You can go right up till the hills; you can proceed on a cross-country tour. The car will not fail you." I trust what they are saying. The manufacturers are great. The car, too, is great. But will this car carry me till the market? I do not doubt you when you tell me that this car can carry me to places far off, to countries I have never seen before, to the seas, to the mountains, to all the unknown places. I trust you when you tell me that this car can carry me without disappointing me. But again I ask you, can this car take me to the nearby market? Because I trust the old one. It was cranky but it delivered. Even if it would fail me, the failure would be a small failure. The distance was just 10 kilometres, so if I had to walk, the walk would be just 10 kilometres. And I knew all the people in the marketplace, so if the car would refuse to start, then there was enough manpower available to push it to the nearest garage.'

That is our situation. If Ashtavakra can help you reach the highest, why do you think he wouldn't suffice to keep you going at least till the marketplace?

It is a very common question. A lady told me, 'With your teachings, my son has gained great wisdom! Now he understands life, now his mind and eyes are very sharp, he is quickly able to read situations, he cannot be fooled, change does not excite or disappoint him, he cannot be lured easily, and he does not get afraid or frustrated easily. Everything about him is now sublime and shiny! But, you know, I have a great doubt, it keeps killing me: Will he be able to earn a livelihood?'

The lady is saying she is assured that her son can earn a place in the heavens, but she is not sure whether he can earn a livelihood. She is saying, 'Now he is sharp and wise, quick and nimble, patient and prolific—but how will he earn a livelihood?'

You know, that is also a sad comment on the means through which most people nowadays earn their livelihood. The lady is saying, 'Yes, he is wise—but how will he earn his livelihood?' You know what she is saying? That livelihood anyway does not come to wise people—it goes to the most foolish of the lot.

But still, don't worry. In detachment there is great energy. One is detached from all the sickness and sloth and sleep. One is detached from sickness, and hence what does one have? Health. If you have detachment from sloth, sleep, and sickness, what are you left with? You are left with great action, nimbleness, speed, and energy. So, don't worry.

It's just that the energy of a common man is random and chaotic energy: it exhibits itself with a lot of unnecessary noise, sound and fury as they say. And that noise, that sound, that exhibition is nothing but a dissipation of energy.

The energy of the wise man is not available for dissipation. It is a silent and well-channelized energy, so you might be in doubt for a while because the exhibition will stop. Excitement, for example, is exhibition of energy. Adrenaline, testosterone, these are all exhibitions of energy, and they only lead to wastage of energy. You will not experience these exhibitions now.

Let the absence of exhibitions not make you think that you have lost on energy itself. Do not conclude erroneously. Energy is there, but now it is silent energy, peaceful energy. It will not be violent; it will be the servant of wisdom. When the occasion arises, you will find that suitable energy has also arisen within you. And when the occasion to act energetically will not be there, you will find that you don't have an unnecessary abundance of energy, as most people have.

Have you seen those people? They are needlessly full of energy. And what is the result? They can't sleep. They can't relax. Even on the bed, your energy will force you to continue doing something. And if there is nothing else to do, you will start doing something with the pillow, or start turning and curving and stretching and swinging, all kinds of antics that can be performed on the bed.

When you will need action, action will happen. And it is great that action will not happen unnecessarily. It is, of course, important that one acts when action is needed, but it is probably even more important that one does not act when action is not needed. Most of the troubles of this world are because people are acting even when there is no need to act.

Look at the roads: people are hurrying, going from here till there, rushing about. Is there really a need for all the action that you see around you and within you? Thought is inner action. Do you really need all that action, happening, within you? Just as one has thoughts within needlessly, one has a lot of action outside needlessly.

So, it is great if the touch of Ashtavakra decapacitates you of needless action.

Now you won't be prone to excitement.

Now nobody will be able to come and unnecessarily charge you up and compel you to act compulsively.

Now you will be a master of yourself.

It is of course important that one acts when action is needed, but it is probably even more important that one does not act when action is not needed.

~

13

How to Bring Spontaneity to Actions

Advait Shivir, Naukuchiatal, 2018

Be an outlier. Be a bit of an eccentric.
Question the obvious. Question the normal. Question
all the accepted norms, modes.

~

Acharya Prashant (AP): Spontaneity and continuity are our nature; they occur to us naturally. Fear impedes spontaneity, and there cannot be fear unless you have lazily convinced yourself that you are dependent, or set to lose much. It is a false conviction; it can occur to you only in lazy belief. If you can be a little more agile, if you can get up and move a little, if you can venture into those areas of your psyche that you take for granted and, therefore, casually ignore, then you will get a chance to re-examine your beliefs. In fact, knowledge about your beliefs will come even before re-examination.

We all operate through very subconscious beliefs. We act without knowing what the foundation, the fundamental driver, the very motive of the action is. We just act, and because we have been acting like that since quite long, we assume that the action is in place, that the action must be right, proper, etc.

We do not know where our actions come from. We do not know where our thoughts come from. And without knowing, we take them as acceptable; we even give them the status of truth.

An impulse arises; we feel like rushing to a certain place. You do not ask yourself, 'Where is this impulse arising from?' What you see is that the same impulse has been present in you since long and that the world around you also appears to be governed by the same impulse, so very lazily you allow yourself to be carried away by it.

As I said earlier, there is too much flab on the mind. It needs to be melted, cut down. You need to move. You need to ask questions. You need to ask uncomfortable questions, you need to ask new questions, you need to ask questions that others may not appear to be asking themselves.

If you are not asking those questions, then you will remain a prisoner to dead habits.

Dead habit does not include spontaneity. Dead habit comes from loads of temporal accumulation of evolutionary residue. That evolutionary residue has helped you survive in a physical sense but nothing more than that. You won't get the simple joy of life if you live from that residue, by that residue. Clearing that residue is perhaps easy. But, first of all, its huge existence has to be acknowledged. We are carrying loads of it.

Just as a fat man becomes used to the physical load that he is carrying—so much so that it stops troubling him to an extent—he even starts calling the unnecessary weight as himself. A man might be carrying a lot of unnecessary weight on his arm, but if you touch that arm, he would not say that you are touching something unnecessary; he will say, 'You are touching me.'

So, there develops an identification with the unnecessary, and all that impedes smooth action, all that just blocks spontaneity, a smooth immediacy. They become the victims.

Everything has to be probed. One has to look at himself quite skeptically. 'Why did you just smile? Where is the smile coming from?' Even simple matters such as these. Because they appear to be simple, we just let them pass. We are not alert enough, agile enough to investigate. That investigation is extremely important. 'Why do I do what I do?' And if you are not careful about small things, then even in the so-called big matters of life you will just lazily be dictated by old habits. Questioning is extremely necessary. There is nothing so sacred that it cannot be questioned. That which is really sacred is anyway not available to be questioned.

So, whatever is available to be questioned must be questioned. And don't feel offended if somebody else questions you. You feel offended when others question you precisely because you have never questioned yourself. Those who do not look honestly at themselves, those who do not want to seek their answers, feel bad when they are questioned by others. If you are questioned by others, feel grateful. But even that gratitude would come only if you see the need to not live in the dark.

Look at the masses. People are going to their offices, somebody is building a house, somebody is travelling abroad, somebody is trying for a job, somebody is in the maternity ward. And we are asking: Why? In fact, all these things appear so normal that 'why' does not even arise. You have to ask, 'What is happening? Why is it happening?' Even more important than 'why' is 'what', because to ask, 'Why is it happening?' you must first of all know what is happening.

We operate very mechanically. One fixes up his car and drives to the office, one buys an insurance policy, one takes an annual vacation, one organizes a weekend get-together, one orders something to eat, one buys jewelry. The question 'What is happening?' does not arise. It *has* to arise. If it doesn't arise, then you are operating against yourself. You will suffer.

Q: How to know whether we are operating from the real centre or from the ego, from the mind?

AP: Ask, 'What is happening?' Attention reveals so much. It is the greatest method. Don't just casually take things for granted. Don't just say that ten people to my left and right are doing the same thing, so it must be done.

Be an outlier. Be a bit of an eccentric.

Question the obvious.

Question the normal.

Question all the accepted mores, modes.

Q: This extra load, this baggage that we are carrying, are we supposed to reduce it gradually, or is there a way to drop it instantly?

AP: First of all, you are just speculating about the baggage. Do you really know the baggage? Knowing the baggage is not very different from dropping it. If you want to talk about dropping it without first knowing it, then you are just groping in the dark; you do not know what to drop, how big it is, and how you are attached to that stuff. Theoretically, you have been told that you are carrying baggage, and you are asking, 'How do I drop it?' The question is: What to drop?

Q: Once you identify the baggage . . .

AP: . . . it is gone. It is gone. The distance between realization and freedom is very, very small. You may even say that they are one. If you have realized, it cannot take long to be free.

Q: How do I handle anxiety?

AP: Anxiety is not a thing. Anxiety is a shadow. If you ask me, 'How to handle a shadow?' I will say, '*Whose* shadow?'

Q: Handle the thing.

AP: Now, whose shadow is anxiety? You will have to tell me. Anxiety is an appearance; anxiety is what comes to you as a result of an unnatural life. Should we talk of the anxiety, or should we talk of the thing that casts the dark shadow?

Q: The thing.

AP: What is that thing?

Q: In everything there is anxiety. For example, waking up at 5 o'clock instead of the usual 10 o'clock for today's morning session created a lot of tension.

AP: It is bad, we cannot live like that.

Q: Anxiety comes with just keeping up the pace. For me, it started in my childhood. Now my son is like that also. He is slow, so I am putting the same pressure upon him which was once put upon me.

AP: *(Points to the woods nearby)* Look at that. There are trees of all shapes and sizes, aren't there? Even the colors vary. Then there is the grass. There is no obligation for the grass to rise like a tree. The grass is all right as the grass. There is no need to match the pace.

Q: But you are useless if you are slow.

AP: Useless in whose eyes?

Q: You will not be valued in life. Nobody will involve you in anything.

AP: Let them not involve you, then!

Q: If you would organize this session, would you involve me even if I am slow?

AP: I will find a very, very suitable use for you. The scooter has a tyre, the jumbo jet, too, has one. It is not the fault of the scooter's tyre that it is designed in a particular way. But foolish is the one who tries to use the scooter tyre in the jumbo jet. They all have their uses. Look at the grass under your feet. Why do you feel that it is useless? What is this entire concept of usefulness? To whom do you want to be useful?

Q: To the world around me.

AP: Seriously? With all the harshness that you have towards yourself, how will you do good to the world?

Q: I am less agile than most.

AP: It is all right. If less is more, then it is a matter of comparison. It is all right.

Q: Don't we need to put effort into developing ourselves?

AP: You see, even physical nature has a pace for everything and respect for everything. Mountain brooks, they are so swift and agile. Glaciers, they languish, they are so slow—as if they are frozen. What is the speed of a glacier? How fast does it move? Extremely slowly. These Himalayan mountains, even they are in motion; they are rising every moment. They are gaining height at the rate of four inches per year; that is their pace. Must the mighty Himalayas be ashamed of themselves?

Most of the swiftness that you see in the world is the result of fear. If a big greyhound comes here, you discover how swift you can be. And that is how most people come to their swiftness: their swiftness is born out of fear. I am not an advocate of slowness or tardiness. I am an advocate of being natural.

You may run very fast, but where are you going? What is the point in going around in circles? All right, circles with progressively increasing radii, but still they are just circles. The small man has a small circle, and the so-called big man has a big circle. But both of them are, nevertheless, just going around in circles. What is the point? And even if you complete the circle faster than the others over and over again, how does it help you? You must be a little friendlier towards yourself. You must ask yourself, 'Is all this helping me?'

The concern for fastness comes from, in this time, the factory model of production. What do you want there? You want stuff that is bigger and faster, and you very well know that most of that is motivated by sheer greed. Can a painter be fast? What if the painter is fast? Would you like to buy a fast painting? Can a cook be fast? We do not want him to be foolishly slow either, but do we want him to be fast? Mostly, this thing about being fast is a thing about rushing. People rush in the name of swiftness. That is why we are all rushed up and hurried.

Q: You just mentioned something about being foolishly slow. What do you mean by 'foolishly slow'?

AP: Being foolishly slow is when something is possible within your natural capacity, to be done at a certain rate, but because of sheer clumsiness and laziness and inertia, you decide to not do it. You very well know that you can do the meals by 8 p.m., but you doze off and wake up at 9:30, and the meals are served at 11 p.m. No one is advocating that. But why would you want to rush up the whole thing? There is bliss to be had in the process of creativity. Why do you want to short-circuit the process?

Q: I become hasty when I do something.

AP: It is because you are trying to catch up with others. Don't try to do that. Be your best self. Ask yourself, 'Am I being lazy?' And if you are being lazy, then do shrug off your laziness and hurry up. But if you are not being lazy, there is no need to get nervous; then you can continue at your inherent pace. There is just this one thing you need to guard against.

Q: Laziness.

AP: Laziness, and if you are not being lazy, then there is no need to curse yourself or feel nervous or ashamed. Ask just this one question:'Have I been dishonest? Have I been lazy? Am I dozing off?' And if you're not dozing off, then don't be harsh on yourself.

Q: How should I listen to you? Should I make any effort for that?
AP: Just listen. Don't listen for the sake of something. Just listen without motive. You should be extremely passive when listening, extremely passive, as if you do not exist.

Q: Is not focus required in order to understand?
AP: No, no. No need to focus or concentrate, no need at all. Just go and collapse. Don't try to concentrate, interpret, or focus, all those things that you do with books. You are not

reading a book. Just be present. You may even get a disturbing feeling that you are not understanding anything. Let that feeling be there.

The spiritual process is not the same as the process of accumulation of knowledge. It is a different thing that happens when you are truly listening to a friend or a teacher. So, just listen. It is quite possible that you may not remember much after the session, but that doesn't matter. Just listen. Then comes the time when you are back to your daily life, your daily chores. Then you have to spring up, then you have to wake up, then you have to be extremely alert and focused towards that one thing that is happening.

So, these are two very different modes of being. In front of the teacher, sit as if you are there to relax. Don't sit as if you are there to gather because gathering is a tension. In tension you will not be able to have spontaneity, freedom, relaxation. There is no understanding possible without relaxing. Only in relaxation does understanding spontaneously and causelessly happen.

But when you are back to the grind of your daily life, then you cannot afford to be loose. Then you have to be tight. Then the seeker has to be tight, he has to be vigilant. He cannot just allow himself to be swayed away, taken away. The forceful flow of impulses and habits is always there, and it can very easily carry you away. It is a very giant flow, like one of the mountainous rivers in this season. How are rivers in the season? Flowing with great force, and if you enter them, you will be . . .?

Q: Swept away?
AP: Yes. That is similar to the inner flow of tendencies. You won't be able to even bat an eyelid: before you open your eyes, you are gone.

So, when you are not in front of a teacher, then you have to ask, 'What is going on, what is going on, what is going on?' A point comes in the spiritual journey when you will be able to afford to drop the vigilance, but that will require some time and practice. Then even in daily life you can relax as you relax in front of the teacher. But right now, given your situation, you have to be extremely vigilant in your daily life.

Q: How do I jump out of this game of happiness and sadness? **AP:** One can take pleasure in this game for a while. One can go down and feel bad, and then one can come up and feel happy. But a point comes when one starts finding this game stupid. One says, 'Why can't I have something uninterrupted? Why can't I have something that is not continuously threatened by the see-saw dynamics? Why is it necessary for me to be down in order to experience being up?' Those who start seeing that happiness is not quite the heaven one takes it to be find something beyond happiness. That something has been called joy.

Joy is to not remain dependent on sadness for happiness.

Joy is to not have intermittent pleasure.

Joy is to be where there is freedom from both happiness and sorrow.

So, the game of happiness and sadness continues, the seesaw, and you are joyful in spite of how the game is unfolding. And the game will definitely involve sometimes sadness, sometimes happiness, but you are all right in either condition. Through the full spectrum, the entire span of the movement of the seesaw, you are unconditionally all right. That is joy.

But to come to joy, you must firstly be fed up with the pursuit of happiness. The world we live in places a huge

premium upon happiness. One has to see through the
ignorance. One has to cut through the maze. One has to see
how the social institutions and the market dynamics are all
designed to trap a human being in the name of happiness.

You must remember that the goal of life is not happiness
but freedom—freedom from both happiness and sadness.

*Joy is to not remain dependent on sadness for happiness. Joy
is to not have intermittent pleasure. Joy is to be where there is
freedom from both happiness and sorrow.*

14

The Right Action Is Its Own Reward

Advait Shivir, BodhSthal, 2017

The mind obsessed with its upkeep, its security, its welfare, its wellbeing, its preservation, its continuity cannot rebel. Only a carefree mind can rebel. Only a faithful mind can rebel. Only an assured mind can rebel.

~

Questioner (Q): It is said that the one who is not able to incorporate the knowing into his doing is worse than the one who does not know at all. Could you give some clarification on this?

Acharya Prashant (AP): You see, man has an active mind. Man has a mind driven by a so-called self-supporting ego. Man is the only creature in existence that feels that he is all by himself. That is why man faces the kind of worries and tensions that no other creature does. You feel greatly responsible for yourself. You feel as if your welfare and upkeep is all upon you.

The mind is small, and it cannot admit anything immense, large, beyond itself. It is not even a matter of intention; it is just impossible for it. The cup cannot conceive of the ocean.

So, one has no faith. The more active and self-supporting the mind becomes, the more faithless it becomes. The more you start living supported by and according to your concepts, ideologies, inventions, constructs, and social orders, the more insecure you become.

You are wearing clothes manufactured by you. You are living in a building made by you. You are following an ideology made by yourself. Even the most intimate affairs of your life—cohabitation, mating, copulation, reproduction—are according to social orders and norms made by . . .?

Q: You.

AP: Even your love is man-made. It is a manufactured love, it is a factory love. There is no possibility of reliance upon anything except yourself.

To really rebel, one has to be very dismissive of the outcome of the rebellion. One must have a mind that says, 'Whatever comes is all right. Whatever comes will be taken care of by something beyond me.'

To really be able to play with life and through life, you must feel secure in the lap of a caring father. We have lost all touch with the one who takes care. According to our limited perception and beliefs, we take care of . . .?

Q: Ourselves.

AP: And we feel we are the only ones who take care of . . .?

Q: Ourselves.

AP: How can you rebel? If you have to take care of yourself, then you have to be very careful. There can be no rebellion in an environment of carefulness. Such carefulness just impedes the flow of rebellious action. It asks you to wait, watch, analyze, compromise. It does not let you have that natural impulse of the mountain spring.

Do you see inhibition there? Ever seen a young river flowing down the hills? Do you see the swiftness, the frictionless movement, the impatience? There are boulders blocking her way, and she is not the one to wait and negotiate. Sometimes she jumps over them, sometimes she makes her way besides them, and when it is in her might, she just breaks through them. But one thing is certain: she will not stay with them. They may stay. She has somewhere to reach.

The river has not yet reached there, but she is so full of sureness. Man has denied himself that unreasonable sureness. If you ask the river, 'How are you so sure that you are doing the right thing? Maybe you are more secure here. You know, the plains are all polluted. The moment you reach the plains, they are going to dump sewage into you!' The river won't listen to you. She will say, 'I will meet my fate, and my fate is not to halt at the hills. I might be polluted, contaminated, raped in the plains, but the plains are the gateway to the sea. If I hate the plains, there is no way I am going to reach the sea.' That is what I am calling as being dismissive of the future, being dismissive of the result.

We are just too careful because we feel that we have to take care of ourselves. We start shivering the moment we feel that the future is not going to be as per our plans. That must have happened with most of you at some point or the other. Oh, I am sure it happens very regularly! What is the point in understating things?

You want your son or daughter to have a certain kind of academic future, and she comes and says, 'Nothing after class twelve, I am done!' Ever seen how the guts start squirming? You must have experienced that. And there can be worse admissions that your son or daughter can make in front of you. Even the sons and the daughters know the reaction they will get when they come out and talk, so often they keep things to themselves.

You have arranged so much money and jewelry for her marriage. One day she comes and says, 'Papa . . .' See how the inner world collapses? Even imagining such a thing makes you go weak in the knees—as if you are so certain that what you have thought of for her is the best thing that could happen!

But man lives in the belief that he knows what is best for himself. 'I will decide how my life should be. I am a self-made man, you see. I don't leave things to chance. I will decide when I will have cancer.' And cancer comes at the exact hour and second and date appointed by you, doesn't it? Doesn't it?

Do what is right and forget all about the result. If the action is right, then the result is right.

The right action cannot have a wrong result. If it appears wrong to you, it is because it is clashing with your beliefs and expectations. It is actually right. The right tree cannot bear the wrong fruit, but it may appear wrong to you if you are expecting mangoes from a guava tree. Guavas, too, have their own beauty, their own sweetness, their own aroma. And the guava tree is not saying that you cannot have mangoes; mango trees, too, are abundant. You can have both guavas and mangoes.

The right action is its own reward. There is no need to split the action from the result of the action. We tend to do that. We say, 'Oh yes, this thing is right, and it must be done, but . . .' If the thing is right and it must be done, from where has this split arrived? What is this 'but'?

Rightness is one. The right action is its own fruit.

Now you can rebel. If rebellion is the right thing to do, why bother about the result of rebelling? Now rebellion is not scarier or even a big event; it just happens.

It is hot in the sun, and you seek shade. Is this rebellion? You are thirsty, and you take some water. Is this rebellion?

What is big or monumental about it? What makes you think ten times about it? It is natural, it is free flowing. It requires no thought, and it entails, involves no violence.

(Points at a rabbit) He is listening carefully. Whenever we have a session, he comes and sits carefully and listens like this. But if you try to disturb him, he will run away and sit somewhere else. He is just rebelling. Rebellion is as smooth as that: sit somewhere else! That is the essence of all rebellion.

That is incidentally also the meaning of the word *sanyāsa*, to be rightly placed. Are you sitting at the wrong place? Sit somewhere else! Be *sanyāsth*. Take *sanyāsa*. When the rabbit leaves this place and goes somewhere else where people are a little less curious about him, then he is just taking *sanyāsa*. *Sanyāsa* is rebellion.

The mind obsessed with its upkeep, its security, its welfare, its wellbeing, its preservation, its continuity, cannot rebel. Only a carefree mind can rebel. Only a faithful mind can rebel. Only an assured mind can rebel.

And that assurance, mind you, does not come from any fact or reason; it is a reasonless, baseless, absurd assurance. As they say, God is *nirādhāra* (without support). It is a *nirādhāra* assurance; it has nothing concrete behind it. It rests on nothing and, therefore, it cannot be shaken. That kind of assurance.

If someone comes and tells you, 'You know what? Your confidence is baseless!' then you must know that you are really confident.

Our confidence is always based on certain things. If those things are taken away, the confidence falls. When you can be confident, just be confident for no reason at all; when you have neither knowledge nor possessions nor anything material to assure you and yet you are so confident, then you have arrived.

There are two kinds of students. If there is a mathematics exam, and you go and stand in front of the examination hall, you will find two kinds of students.

There are the ones who have really mugged up the theorems and have really practised the sums, and, therefore, they are confident. They have gone through the syllabus over and over again. They have seen the past years' question papers and predicted what is likely to appear in this year's paper, so they are confident.

Now, if the question paper changes pattern, if there is something out of syllabus, if there is something that does not match with their expectations, then all the confidence evaporates; then they start shivering. They had prepared so much, and the preparation is of no use now. Such confidence is the confidence that mankind has. If a man has money, then he is all puffed up. He looks so sure. What if the money is gone? Our confidence is always reasonable.

Then there is another student who just knows mathematics. At most, he has memorized a few formulae—at most. Even the formulae he can actually derive from the basic principles, so he does not need to even remember that much. He works from the first principles. He has not mugged up a textbook. His certainty does not come from rehearsals and practise. He just knows mathematics. He has become one with the language of mathematics. Mathematics is not something artificial; it is the language of existence. It is happening all the time. This fellow has now started understanding that language, speaking that language. He will not depend on a particular paper format. You can keep changing the formats, the sections, the time duration; objective questions can change to subjective questions and such things. This fellow is undaunted.

This is real confidence, confidence that proceeds from nowhere, *nirādhāra*. 'I am just confident. Take away everything that I have, and I would still be confident.' Such confidence is called faith. If you don't have this confidence, then life is not worth living. You will be all the time shivering in insecurity. You will be all the time trying to protect something or the other.

Rebellion happens when you just have confidence. If you rebel, what is the worst that can happen to you? Everything can be taken away, but you would still remain confident. You haven't been harmed. 'My welfare does not depend on things. My welfare does not depend on possessions or knowledge or relationships. I am just all right.'

Now you can rebel because, well, you have nothing to lose. You can lose everything and yet stay perfect. 'I am already and simultaneously at the climax and at the nadir. How am I at the climax?'

Q: Internally confident . . .

AP: 'I am perfect. And how am I at the zeroth level? I don't have anything to lose! I have already lost everything.'

That is the condition of the Buddha. That is the liberated man. Simultaneously at the peak and at the lowest point of the valley.

Do what is right and forget all about the result. The right action cannot have a wrong result. If it appears wrong to you, it is because it is clashing with your beliefs and expectations. It is actually right. The right tree cannot bear the wrong fruit.

15

If Bad Karma Gets a Bad Reward, Why Do We Still Act Badly?

With IIT Kharagpur, 2020

The right action is action that brings peace and relaxation to you. It leads to a diminishing of the inner uncertainty and anxiety. The right action leaves you with reasonless contentment.

~

Questioner (Q): You have said, 'The right action is its own reward, the wrong action is its own punishment.'

Based on this quote, we should always favour the right action and be averse to the wrong action, but usually we do just the opposite. Kindly throw some light on this.

Acharya Prashant (AP): To whom are these rewards or punishments coming? You have to understand this. If someone has lived an entire lifetime based on wrong decisions, wrong actions, then what is it that has started appearing 'right' to this person?

Before we proceed, we must revisit what right action or decision means.

The right action is action that brings peace and relaxation to you. The right action leaves you with reasonless contentment. It leads to a diminishing of the inner uncertainty and anxiety. That is right action, and that also conversely defines wrong action.

So, the right action brings peace to you. But what if you are someone whose entire life is built on a sequence of wrong actions? You have become totally conditioned, totally acclimatized. You have invested a lot in the wrong. The wrong has strongly started appearing right to you. Now, when you make a truly right decision, what comes to you is the truly right reward, but that right reward is incompatible with your pre-existing life structure, so you suffer.

This explains why people avoid the right action. People avoid the right action because it is incompatible with the entire structure of their life.

People do not operate from a clean slate. Were people operating from a clean slate, from a zero-base with no past, no biases, no carry-overs whatsoever, then everybody would have chosen in favour of the right action and decision. But people have a history, and that history is often full of wrongness. Not only have we lived wrongly in the past but we have also raised great stakes in what is wrong. Now we are caught, stuck.

Now, even if we accidentally make a right decision, it comes as a jolt to all that we have, it shakes up our foundations. Even though it is the best thing that can happen to us, that right thing, that best thing comes to us accompanied by a lot of suffering.

Remember, the right thing is not bringing suffering to us; the suffering is because we have lived wrongly so far. But how would it appear on the surface? It would appear that life was smooth, there was hardly any suffering, and then I deviated from my normal course, took a so-called right decision, and that right decision has brought unnecessary suffering to me.

So, what does one do? One drops the right and one goes back to his dated, pre-existing ways. The reward indeed did arrive, but we did not like the reward; the reward was uncomfortable.

There is this kid, and the kid has been playing in mud. All drenched, the kid comes back. The right thing to happen to the kid is that he is put in the bathtub, and then scrubbed, shampooed. That's the right thing. But this right thing will make him uncomfortable, and he was very comfortable with all the mud and dust sticking to him, plastered to his body, was he not? There was a stink arising from his clothes, but he had grown used to it over four–five hours. After playing in the mud for so long, he was tired. He wanted to sleep, but the mother picked him up, put him in the bath, and the scrubber was really hurting, and some of the shampoo entered his eyes and the eyes burnt.

So, the reward did come. If you are so unclean, is cleanliness not a reward? The right action is its own reward. What was the right action? Taking a bath was the right action. What is the reward? Cleanliness is the reward. So, the reward definitely came, but the reward made the person uncomfortable.

Now you know why people choose the wrong even though the right thing definitely brings its own reward. Who likes that reward? We are lazy people. And often dirty too. Lazy and dirty. Think of the kid. The kid is dirty and feeling too lazy to take a bath. That's how most of us are, right?

Now, look at the wrong action in the same condition. The wrong action is: 'Yes, you can go and happily sleep now. You can go and happily sleep and spoil the bed sheet and the pillow covers as well.'

Now, the wrong action has come along with punishment. What is the punishment? One, you will keep stinking. Second, your skin will suffer. Third, you have spoiled the bed sheet and the pillow and everything. But this wrong action is something the kid will feel quite happy and comfortable with.

So, the punishment is there. But what if you start liking the punishment?

Think of an imagined and an ideal scenario. If the kid is not yet drenched in mud and he is given an option, 'Do you want to stay clean or do you want to stay dirty?' what would he choose? He would choose cleanliness. From a neutral position, he would definitely go for the right thing because he has not yet invested in the wrong thing. Because he does not yet have a history, he is at point zero, time zero. At time zero, it is quite likely, quite possible to take the right decision.

Please understand that none of us operate from a clean slate, from point zero. We have a history, and the history has become us. That is what is called conditioning. Your history takes your name. You are no more a free being. You are somebody who is determined by his history. And if you are determined by your history, then it requires discipline and determination to take the right action.

The temptation to take the wrong action is very high. Most people succumb to that temptation. You should not.

When you make a truly right decision, what comes to you is the truly right reward, but that right reward is incompatible with your pre-existing life structure, so you suffer.

16

In the Right Battle, Defeat Is Victory

Myth Demolition Tour, Rishikesh, 2020

*Carry the spirit of victory even in your defeat. That is a
bigger victory than victory.*

~

Questioner (Q): My question is about renunciation. I see that
I want to do things like renunciation and living in poverty,
but I go in the opposite direction. I never find the bravery to
really do what I want to do. When I will be ready to do this
renunciation that I know I have to do?

Acharya Prashant (AP): What is it that you want to renounce?

Q: The world of the senses. I still care about the external
and the material world. However, I see no meaning in that
material world, but at the same time, I don't have the strength
to say that I've had enough.

AP: What do you mean by this word, 'poverty'?

Q: The way I understand it, poverty means doing work like
cleaning the streets in order to make the ego weak. The
ego won't like cleaning the streets, so I will do it to reduce
the ego. I like St. Francis of Assisi very much, and I see
that some saints go this way of serving others because it is
the direction towards God somehow. The other direction
is ego, which is the opposite direction. But this ego inside

of me is strong. I don't know when I will be ready, how many lives or . . .

AP: It may not really require many lives.

There is the direction of renunciation, and there is the direction of possession and identification and attachment. Obviously, you must do your best to decide in the favour of the right direction. But as you said, many times your old tendencies would overpower you, compel you to identify with the world and feel one with it.

So, two things. One, even if your defeat is to come, let it be a hard-fought defeat. Do your best to make the right choice, do your best to move in the right direction. And after doing all that you can—and there is really a lot that you can do—if you are still forcibly pulled towards the other direction, the direction of indiscretion, the direction of blind material pull, then at least you should know that you fought honestly.

That is the first thing. Do not give in easily. And if you do not give in easily, you will find that you are capable of far more than you might usually think of.

Then the second thing. When you choose rightly, when you win, that is obviously a welcome and auspicious situation. So, no need to talk about that situation because in that situation you would have already done what should have been done. So, chapter closed. The right thing has been done.

It still remains to be discussed what to do when one has not been able to choose rightly, when one has been made to side with the world. When one knows fully well that one is not on the right side of spirituality or *Dharma* (duty for liberation), what to do then?

You have been pulled to the wrong camp, right? That's the situation in those moments. You have been pulled to the wrong side. Now, observe clearly what is there on that side. You now belong to a place—even if temporarily, momentarily—that you should not have belonged to in the first place. But what to do? We are all mortal creatures in flesh and blood. We all have our flaws, our weaknesses, our indiscretions.

Now, let's say, for an evening, we belong to the wrong place. What to do? Don't just keep cursing yourself. Observe. Ask yourself: 'There surely was something in this place that attracted me so much. What was it? There surely is some power in this place that defeated me. What is that power?' Now that you have been forced to come to the wrong place, at least investigate it properly. Let it be some kind of a spy mission. That is the best use you can put your defeat to.

I should have been in my study at this time. I should have been with the hills or with the river or at the church at this time. And where am I? I am at a shopping complex or at a liquor party. Theoretically, I very well know I shouldn't have been here at this moment, but I am here, and I can't change the fact of my presence at this place. So, what do I then make of this evening? Study that place. Study that place so that your defeat does not get repeated. That place surely has some power. That place surely has some charm that speaks to some weakness within you. Study that charm. What is it in that place that compels you? Is that charm for real?

Often the charm is imaginary, and when you go close to it, it disappears. So, maybe the image of the charm sucked you in. But now that you are there, now that you have indeed been sucked in, use the opportunity and really see whether the charmer is worth it. What else can be done anyway? You are there. You are not with the hills, you are not with the river, you are not with the books, you are not with the saints. You are at that blitzy, blingy party.

So, that is the best use you can put your defeat to. And that is very important for all of us because we will get defeated. Some of us will get very frequently defeated, the others maybe a little less frequently, but there is nobody who is an absolute winner. We all have our moments, our episodes of failures. We all let ourselves down some time or the other. What to do then? Keep fighting.

What was rule number one? Do not go down tamely. If there is an inner conflict and you know which side should win, fight hard to ensure that the right side prevails. That was rule number one.

Rule number two: Even when you are defeated, keep fighting. Now, of course, frontal warfare is not possible. The direct and obvious battle has been lost, so let there be guerrilla warfare now.

The enemy has pulled you to his camp. Now what do you do? Spy. Surveillance. Act as a detective on yourself. 'So, this is the place that overpowered me. What exactly is so enthralling about it? Let me figure out. He is the man who did not allow me to be at a place of peace; something about him just overwhelmed me. What is it about that man? I will not just stay at a seductive distance and allow his charm to continue. I will go close to him. I will figure out whether he is really worth it.'

Either you ensure that you remain a long distance away from him—that would be your absolute victory—but if you cannot do that, if he indeed does pull you towards himself, then go totally towards him. Investigate. And if your investigation is honest, the charm will disappear. And if the charm does not disappear even upon really rigorous examination, then maybe the person is worth it! *(Laughs)* There is no need to run away then. Maybe the one pulling you in, his himself a saint in some other form. Fine. If you have a living saint, why do you need to go to a library or some such place?

Keep fighting. Keep fighting till your victory, and keep fighting in your defeat. The second part is more important. Keep fighting even when you have been beaten down. Keep fighting even when yours looks like a hopeless cause, a lost battle. Don't just start wallowing in self-pity and self-abuse. 'Oh, I am such a wretched one! I betrayed God, my Lord!' You did not betray Him; you did what you could. Now continue doing what you can. That's the thing: continuity. Surprise the enemy. Let him think that he has won. And even when it appears that he has won, you must continue fighting. There is no other option.

Even when you have been taken prisoner by the other camp, continue fighting. Good if you have been taken prisoner! You have been allowed access to the other camp. That's a great opportunity to just blast yourself off and bring down the entire enemy camp along with yourself, no? He thinks he is bringing in a prisoner—you should know that he is bringing in a suicide bomber! Continue fighting.

There are enough tales in India on the same theme. There are so many tales that you cannot tell them apart, so even in my mind there is a mishmash of all those tales. I will try to narrate the mishmash to you.

So, there is that all-powerful king, very powerful king—as tales go, they all have some powerful king—and then there is this very beautiful girl in his kingdom. And the girl has been brought up by her father who is a devoted priest, so she has been brought up the best way possible: even though she is physically quite charming, her mind is totally in the Truth. She has mastered the scriptures at a young age, she engages in debates, she writes, she paints, she sings. She is a beautiful person in the innermost sense, and obviously she has no interest in marriage and such things.

One day, the king is out on a fun trip killing animals and he happens to find this girl. He does what kings do. He sends over for her father and says, 'I want to marry your daughter.' Father says, 'But she's not one for marriage.' Again, the same hackneyed story. The king says, 'Your head would be found rolling on the ground within the next minute if you try to refuse my command.' Father says, 'You can kill me but I will not force my daughter.' The daughter comes to learn of all this, and she tells her father, 'Father, there is no need to get killed. I will marry the king.'

At this point in the story, it looks like the king has won. The authority of the king has prevailed, the physical, material power of the king has prevailed, and the girl has succumbed, right? The girl has succumbed. So bad!

She gets married to the king. And the king initially does what a powerful man is likely to do: he feasts on her body. But slowly, she starts delivering education to him in hidden ways. The king is not somebody who would easily listen to the scriptures or words of wisdom. So, in some way or the other, she starts talking sense to the king. She does not allow her centre to be displaced. Even in the king's palace, she continues with her practices, her *sādhanā* (spiritual practice), her reading, her austerities, everything. Externally, the king has possessed her. Internally, she remains totally untouched, a virgin.

And then, in due course of time, it is found that the king starts developing an interest in the Truth, in the scriptures. He starts coming to her not so much for physical pleasures but to get taught. Initially, he does not admit that he wants his wife to teach him—too much for the masculine ego—but slowly, with her patience, the king starts melting.

A point comes when he clearly accepts that he wants to be her disciple rather than her husband. It might have taken a decade or so, I do not know. There is no such story actually, so how can I know? Then comes a day when she is walking back to her father's place—which is probably an ashram—with the king following in her footsteps.

So, there was a day when the king had forcibly abducted her from her place, and then comes a day when she is going to her place, and the king is obediently walking behind her. So, it happens.

There is a great scripture called *Tripurā Rahasya* (The mystery beyond the Trinity). It is in a little bit of a similar setting with the wife instructing the husband.

Continue your fight even when it appears totally lost. Do not just come up with excuses. Defeat is such a great excuse to remain defeated. 'Oh, I am defeated!' The moment this becomes an excuse, you will remain defeated. Now your defeat will become permanent.

So, never say that you are defeated. Let there be setbacks but be convinced of your ultimate victory. Know for sure that if you are siding with the Truth, then the victory is already yours. Therefore, all defeats are bound to be merely temporary. That sureness has to be there. That is called faith.

There is nobody, I repeat, who is not going to face adversities or reverses. It is your response to those moments that will decide your fate. In victory, everybody is a champion. You must be a champion even in defeat. That is what is needed. It is a bit of a bravado thing. Quite dramatic. You remember that classic reply of King Porus to Alexander?

So, Alexander came to India, like he went to other places in Asia, with the intent to conquer and plunder. Persia had already been subjugated, and he was now knocking on the doors of India. King Porus was at that time ruling a territory that was broadly in today's Punjab. In fact, a little west of today's Punjab. That was the gateway to India. Porus was the first king Alexander needed to conquer if he wanted to penetrate into India.

Alexander had a huge army, and India was divided into a large number of small kingdoms. Compared to Alexander, Porus was a small ruler with a small army, but he fought extremely bravely. But, as was probably inevitable, he was defeated. And then his hands were tied, and he was presented in front of the victorious Alexander, and Alexander asks him, 'So, Porus, how should we behave with you?' And in that moment when all has been lost, his army is destroyed, his kingdom gone, and he is standing with his limbs tied, Porus replies with his head held high, 'As a king behaves with another king.'

It was such a stunning reply. As if the fellow has never been defeated at all! Alexander returned. He dropped his intention to march further into India.

Carry the spirit of victory even in your defeat. That is a bigger victory than victory.

Maya wants to destroy your morale, crush your spirit. Let that not happen. Let her defeat you materially but never spiritually. Let your spirit never be conquered. That is one thing *Maya* has no control over. She has all control over situations, she has all control over your thoughts, tendencies, emotions, but she can have no control really over your faith. Let that remain untouched. That is possible.

Remember, it is not situations that defeat you. Situations are just situations. A situation by definition is something outside of you, whereas a defeat is something inside of you. Situations can at worst be adverse, and a situation is always external. The sense of defeat is an internal thing. That should not come to you.

You are not asking for something small, remember; you are asking for renunciation. Man is not born to renounce. The way our physical and mental constitution is, we are born to stay cursed. It is as if our body and our mind have hatched a foolproof conspiracy against ourselves. There is nothing in us that is really conducive towards liberation. All the senses, they remain so fond of the world; the mind keeps thinking only of the world; the body feeds on the world and exists in the world. So, how is it possible for the person to renounce the world?

Remember that renunciation is really a very high goal. It is a very improbable thing that you are asking for. And when you ask for something so very exquisite, then you should not expect easy attainment. Were you asking for something run-of-the-mill, easy, cheap, then you could have expected it to be achieved in one shot tomorrow. 'Tomorrow, I will try and get it, renunciation, liberation, all those things. Tomorrow itself, yes! Around 8:00 a.m. in the morning maybe, before I finish my breakfast, I will be liberated!'

But fortunately, liberation is not something so valueless; it will demand all of yourself. And it is guaranteed that there would be a lot of defeats in the process. Relish those defeats. What is it to relish those defeats? Even in defeat, remain a winner. 'I have been defeated, but the defeat is not final. If I stay alive, I am going to try. If I don't stay alive, I can't say—maybe I will still try!'

Keep fighting till your victory, and keep fighting in your defeat. Keep fighting even when you have been beaten down. Keep fighting even when yours looks like a hopeless cause, a lost battle. Don't just start wallowing in self-pity and self-abuse.

17

What Is Desireless Action?

Myth Demolition Tour, Rishikesh, 2019

The doing is not for some objective outside of itself;
the doing itself is the objective. This is niśkāma-karma
(desireless action).

~

Questioner (Q): How will I get motivation to work if I am not attached to the result of the work?
Acharya Prashant (AP): When you come to this hall, you are probably prompted by some desire, aren't you?

Q: Yes.
AP: There are desires, there are calculations, there are pluses and minuses. You probably weigh the pros and cons. All those things are there. Sometimes there is a nagging question that you want to get rid of, therefore you come. That is how the thing mostly starts.

So, this is *sakāma-karma* (action with desire for results). Your movement to this hall is motivated by a desire. You want something, therefore you do. This is the common *sakāma-karma*. You do because you want, so the action is a means of fulfilling the desire. This is normal *sakāma-karma*. That's how things are at noon. You are sitting ready to fire your questions. You have a purpose in being here. What is the purpose? 'I want my questions answered.' You have a definite purpose. That's noon.

Now, how is it like at 1:30 p.m.? You came with a question, but the question has not reached here *(points to his desk)*. You do not even intend to ask the question anymore. At noon, when you were listening, you were listening with an objective. What was the objective? The resolution of the query. And how are you listening at 1:30 p.m.? You are just listening. You are *just* listening.

Something is still happening, but the objective is lost. Now the happening itself is very juicy. Now the happening is not a means towards an end; the means itself has merged with the end. It is as if the means has moved into the end or the end has come to the means to bless it. Now there is no distinction. Now you are not saying that let the others' questions be answered fast so that the speaker may take up my question. Hence, now there is no gap. Hence, now there is no waiting for the result. Hence, now time has stopped for you.

This is *niṣkāma-karma* (desireless action). The doing is not for some objective outside of itself; the doing itself is the objective.

What do you work for? You work for some kind of satisfaction, call it deep contentment. You work for the sake of that. Therefore, work is never very satisfying because work to you is not the last thing; the work is just a middleman for the sake of a result. Therefore, work is just a necessary evil for you. Had it been possible, you would've removed the work, the process, the time interval from between, and you would've said, 'Is it possible to come directly to the result?'

That is why man wants to keep gaining in efficiency. Do you see what this continuous movement towards more and more efficient processes, machines, and systems is? It is because man works for a purpose. It is because the work and the time invested in the work is itself not very likable. So, man says, 'Minimize work, and maximize the result'.

Niśkāma-karma means: work is life.

Work is life, anyway. Even when you think you are not working, you are actually working. So, no point fooling oneself with the effort to minimize work. Even when you think you are in a state of leisure, you are actually working. Therefore, why not work in a way that transcends work? That is *niśkāma-karma*.

Work cannot be avoided. Life is work. You are working even when you are sleeping. You are working even when you think you are relaxing. Why not choose work with such deep discretion that work no more remains a load that you have to reduce, something that you want to outsource? Why not come to a situation where you are no longer seeking happiness in the reduction of work?

Have you seen how the common man celebrates when his work burden is reduced? That is *sakāma-karma*. Have you seen how students like to achieve results without working? Were it possible to somehow achieve hundred per cent marks without labouring at all, students would've been the happiest because as a student or as a worker, you find no joy in the process. For you, and for most people, joy is a destination. That is *sakāma-karma*.

And now we will come to the more horrifying part of it: Whenever work is a means to an end, the end is never really achieved. We are beaten both ways! First of all, we expended a lot of time trying to reach an end, and even if we somehow manage to reach that end, what do we discover? 'Eh? Is *this* where I wanted to reach?' And then you proceed towards another destination, and that is what is called the . . .?

Q: Vicious cycle?

AP: So, those who work towards an end find that they are defeated both in the work as well as in the end. Double defeat.

And those who work without an end, those who work because the work itself is service and devotion, they win doubly: First of all, work is celebration; secondly, work is the end.

So, you are celebrating your way to success. You are dancing towards victory. You are dancing not towards victory; you are dancing *in* victory. You are continuously victorious, and you are continuously celebrating.

Compare this to the picture of the one who is striving, toiling, fighting with the dream of some distant success in his eyes. Remember that the success that he dreams of is merely his concept. It is an image because he has not yet come to it. Therefore, the success he is talking of is merely an image. When you come to it, you find that it simply does not match your expectations. Double defeat. First of all, you are striving, toiling, and making life hell for yourself— though with the pride, with the vanity that you are a fighter, that you are a warrior. You will have that satisfaction. So, it may keep egging you on for a very long time, probably even your entire lifetime.

Q: So, it is all about the journey, not the destination?

AP: The destination is everything, but the destination cannot be distant. The destination has to be the first step in the journey. It is not as if it is about the journey and not the destination. Obviously, the destination comes first; the journey begins upon reaching the destination.

So, reach the destination first, and then keep travelling. Destinations upon destinations. Do not travel as if the destination is elusive and far away.

Q: How to make my work an act of devotion?
AP: The work has to be worthy of devotion, first of all. Therefore, choose your work very, very carefully, every day.

Q: Is it a matter of discretion?
AP: Obviously. It is not the work; it is the destination that is commanding the work.

So, what is the work that you are talking of? That is what you must look at. The destination has to be absolutely compelling, so very compelling that you cannot even entertain the thought that it is distant. If you want something really desperately, do you want it five years hence or right now?

Q: Right now.
AP: The destination has to be that attractive. Not only very attractive, but it also has to be that indispensable.

Those who work without an end, those who work because the work itself is service and devotion, they win doubly: First of all, work is celebration; secondly, work is the end.

What Is One's Real Duty?

Advait Shivir, BodhSthal, 2019

There are no duties in life. Life is a duty. Life is either a duty or the most unbearable perdition. That duty has been classically called as Dharma.

Questioner (Q): On being asked if we should do our duty or not, Ramana Maharshi says, 'Yes, certainly. Even if you try to not do your duty, you will be obliged to do it perforce. Let the body complete the task for which it came into being.'

Shri Krishna also says in the Gita, whether Arjuna liked it or not, that he would be forced to fight: 'When there is work to be done by you, you cannot keep away nor can you continue to do a thing when you are not required to do.'

Acharya Prashant (AP): Duty—what is 'duty'?

'When there is work to be done, you cannot keep away.' What is meant by 'work'?

'Nor can you continue to do a thing when you are not required to do.' What is meant by 'requirement'?

We will speak on these.

Does the word 'duty' apply to machines? Does it? Aren't machines doing something or the other all the time? That is what they are designed for. But does the word 'duty' apply to them? Have you ever scolded a machine for neglecting its duty? Imagine somebody scolding his bike or a steam iron. Between the two, I would prefer to be with the steam iron!

Similarly, are animals supposed to do their duty? Does the concept of duty apply to animals? None of us ever thought that Golu, Sumsher, and all the other rabbit chaps *(referring to rabbits at the Advait BodhSthal)* could ever be assigned duties, did we? They just are. They do a lot but they never perform duties.

How is it so that man has duties? What is the fundamental difference? Surely, it has to be the difference between man and animal. Probably, it is duties that make a man a man. If the difference between an animal and a human being is the difference in terms of consciousness—man has a consciousness that asks for expansion, for understanding, for liberation, and the animal has no yearning for that—then, surely, duties must have something to do with consciousness and, therefore, understanding, expansion, and liberation. Isn't that straightforward? Animals, too, have consciousness but their consciousness never demands understanding or salvation or freedom. Do they demand these things? They don't. They are conscious but in their own limited, physical way.

That opens up a way to understand the very principles of duties. Man's duty is to take his consciousness to its pinnacles. That is your only duty. That is your central duty that expresses itself in the form of diverse minor duties. And, therefore, that is the way to test whether you are duty-bound to do something or not. Somebody comes and tells you, 'Do this, you are duty-bound.' How do you test whether that particular thing or action is really a duty for you or not? Test it on your central principle: your central duty is to gain liberation. That is your central duty because you are a human being.

So, when something is touted to you as your duty, ask yourself, 'Will this take me to liberation?' If it will take you to liberation, it is your duty. Otherwise, it is not.

Now, the moment you apply that test to the great set of duties imposed on you, you find that most of these so-called duties go out the window. 'Son, it is your duty to get married for the sake of your grand-grand-grandmother!' Now, will it take you to liberation? No. Will it take her to liberation? She doesn't even want that! How is it a duty, then?

'It is your duty to fight for the honour of your tribe!' Will it take you to liberation? No. How is it a duty, then? Such a dangerous, extremely dangerous touchstone. Because this shows to you that most of your duties are unnecessary, false, and drains on your precious energy and time. You are just wasting your life fulfilling these duties. Not only are you wasting your life but you are also ignoring your real duty by remaining engrossed in all these false and junk duties. By accepting something frivolous as your duty, you are discarding your real duty.

In fact, the real duty is so demanding that it leaves you with no spare energy for any frivolous ones. You cannot have both. You cannot say, 'Okay, fine. I will fulfil my real duty. At the same time, I will just, you know, participate in some frivolous duties.' You cannot do both. Your real duty demands 100 per cent of your being, time, energy, and resources. Not even 0.1 per cent of your being can be spared.

Anything that you divert towards something false is a drain, a task, a diversion from the real thing. Take something away from the real thing and your real purpose suffers. And if the real thing demands 100 per cent of you, then even 99.9 per cent won't suffice. How safe are you if your plane has fuel just enough to cover 99.9 per cent of the journey? The journey, by the way, is 12,000 kilometres. How much is that remaining 0.1 per cent? Merely a few kilometres. How safe are you? You are completely unsafe.

It is either 100 per cent or death. That is the thing with life. Anybody, anything, any misconception that is occupying even 0.1 per cent of yourself is a fatal distraction. To reach the Absolute, you have to offer yourself absolutely, which means 100 per cent. You cannot offer yourself partially and still hope to reach the Absolute. Is the Absolute partial? No. Then how can you make a part payment and obtain it?

Therefore, the worst situation is of those who make 99.9 per cent of the payment because the same fate awaits you whether you pay 99.9 per cent or 0.9 per cent: you will not gain deliverance. And if you are not to gain deliverance, why bother paying 99.9 per cent? You are better off not paying anything at all.

But because here I see you as a set of people who have already paid a lot, who have probably paid 60 per cent, 70 per cent, I would encourage you to go all the way, the full monty. That which you have paid will not return to you now, right? It is gone, it is a sunk cost. Now that you have already paid 70 per cent, it is better to truthfully and honestly make the remaining 30 per cent payment as well and take the delivery. What is the point in paying 70 per cent and getting nothing in return? Remember, there are no refunds. Oh! Too bad. No refunds at all!

The worst situation is of those spiritual seekers, I repeat, who pay 90 per cent, 95 per cent, and get nothing at all. (Smiling) Scary, scary. And that is why you often find completely worldly people less miserable than the so-called spiritual people. Because the completely worldly people paid only to the extent of 5 per cent, their disappointment and frustration is not much. They didn't get anything, but then, they also didn't pay anything. The spiritual person has paid a lot, but because he has not paid in full, because he has not paid in absolute, so he does not get anything, and, therefore, his frustration is great.

There are no duties in life. Life is a duty.

Life is either a duty or the most unbearable perdition. That duty has been classically called as *Dharma*. What is the duty? *Dharma*.

The word 'religion' has become very stained. But religion is nothing but a name for living a real, truthful life of duty. Remember that you must not live for pleasure; you must live to fulfil your duty. You are not alive in order to enjoy life; it is a very false notion. And this kind of a hedonist notion has been implanted deeply in our mind, especially in the last hundred years or so: that you are born to enjoy and all that. No, sir. Sorry! I know I am spoiling the fun for you, but you aren't born to enjoy. Pull that thing out of your head, and now wrap your head around the real centre, wrap your head around your duty. We exist to fulfil our central duty. And what is the central duty?

Q: Liberation?

AP: Truth, liberation, understanding, you know all those words. In fact, those words are so clichéd; I am sometimes wary of using them. But what to do? We don't have too many words for the real thing.

Never complain, 'Oh, but there is so little pleasure in my life!'

Friend, who advised you, first of all, that you will have pleasure in your life?

But you make such a long face and give up such a deep squeal: 'But I don't have happiness!'

Why must you have happiness? Who told you that you did such a great thing by being born, that you will be now rewarded with happiness?

'But all the movies, all the shops, and all the gurus have been telling me that I deserve to be happy! In fact, some of them have been telling me that I am already happy!'

One in particular makes his ends meet just by convincing everybody that they don't exist at all: 'You don't exist at all and you are already the liberated Ātman. Now, go and have a spicy masala dosa!'

Duty is what we live for. Only the liberated one can just live. In our eyes, we are not liberated, so we must live for something. To live for something is your duty; to live for the real thing is your real duty. That is what Shri Krishna is telling Arjuna. 'You cannot just do anything random. You are looking left, you are looking right, sometimes you are talking to the horses, two minutes back you were trying to hide under the chariot, before that you said that you needed to take a washroom break. You have to fight, son. You have to fight. This is a battlefield. And right now, you are not fighting for your personal gain or wealth or kingdom; you are fighting to establish Truth in the kingdom. In front of you are the monstrous powers of evil. Look at that chap Duryodhana, see how he grimaces, and that wannabe rapist Dushasana. You want to hand over the kingdom to them? And they will have that able wizard Shakuni to guide them. Is it these kinds of people you want to trust with running the affairs of the kingdom? It is not about you, Arjuna; it is about a million other people. You have to fight.'

Arjuna is saying, 'No, you see, today is Wednesday!'

So?

'No, it starts with "w".'

So?

'It is very edgy.'

So?

'I am feeling edgy.'

So?

'I won't fight!'

I mean, the general kind of arguments that we all give. And when we give such arguments, we all feel that we are very justified. But that is the nature of our arguments. 'W' has so many edges, doesn't it? Spikes and spikes and spikes; one, two, three.

'I am feeling spooked! I won't fight.'

And why don't you fight?

'The horses are so smelly—I am allergic to such a smell! I won't fight.'

Krishna is saying, 'You hold your horses first, I will take care of these horses, but your internal horses are all going berserk. You don't have the luxury of coming up with such colourful arguments. You have to fight. You are duty-bound, Pārtha.'

That is *Dharma*. We live for the sake of *Dharma*. There is no reason to exist at all. Man lives for the sake of *Dharma*. And if he doesn't live for *Dharma*, his life is the worst perdition. So, fight. You cannot run away. You can almost figuratively see Krishna holding Arjuna by one arm, and this fellow is trying to somehow escape away. He is in no mood to fight.

After the war is over, after all the Kauravas are done and dusted, one day he comes to Krishna and says, 'You know, a little secret: I have totally forgotten the Gita!' Then Krishna is seriously angry. I am not making it up! That is the reason why we are having *Uttara Gita* discourses these days. That's how the *Uttara Gita* begins: Shyly, Arjuna confesses to Krishna, 'You know, Krishna, I really didn't get much of what you said that day. In fact, I don't even know how I won the war. It was all because of you. But now that I am soberer, would you want to repeat a bit of what you were so eloquent with that day?'

You don't exist to make merry. You don't exist to have a rave party on New Year's Eve. I know many of you are planning it, I have my sources. That's not what we are here for.

Know your duty and give yourself totally to it. Will there be pleasure? No, sir, not at all. There would be something higher than pleasure, more fulfilling, more satisfying than pleasure. Pleasure is a turncoat: today one thing, tomorrow another thing. The one who lives by his duty, his *Dharma*, is rewarded with something far higher, far more dependable than pleasure. Those who have known have sometimes called it *mukti* (freedom), sometimes *ānanda* (bliss). Again, there are not too many words for it, but the thing is real. Try it.

When something is touted to you as your duty, ask yourself, 'Will this take me to liberation?' If it will take you to liberation, it is your duty. Otherwise, it is not.

PART III

ACTION THAT REFORMS THE ACTOR

19

What Matters More: The Action or the Actor?

With IIT Kharagpur, 2020

Action can be deceptive: to hide himself or to project a particular kind of image, the actor can indulge in deceptive action.

~

Questioner (Q): At one place you say, 'To know your intentions, watch your actions,' but at another place you say, 'Action does not matter, the actor does.'

I see a contradiction here. Kindly clarify.

Acharya Prashant (AP): When I say, 'To know your intentions, watch your actions,' I want you to be guarded against the hypocrisy of the ego. The ego loves to carry images of everything. It lives in imaginations, it has no Truth, so all that it has is images. It has images of everything, and obviously it has an image of itself as well. The ego thinks: 'This is how I am, this is what I want,' and it obviously carries a self-concept that is conducive to its own survival. That is all that the ego wants. It wants to keep fattening; it wants to continue in time. Survival is its aim.

So, the ego carries an image, and obviously it is a false self-image. How do we challenge this image? How do we know that this image is false? By seeing what it is that we are actually doing, how it is that we are actually living, and there we will usually find a gap, a dissonance.

We might keep thinking to ourselves that we are quite brave, but when we are forced to look at life, our decisions, that is, when we discover that there is hardly any bravery evident in our actions, in our choices. If you do not look at your life, you can happily keep imagining for a long time that you are the bravest one on Earth.

How do I discover that the ego is living in deliberate falseness about itself? By seeing my choices, my actions. So, I say, 'Watch your actions.' That is where you will discover that you are living in falseness, or you will discover that all is well about you.

And then, when I say, 'Actions do not matter, the actor does,' what I mean to say is that when you are to decide upon an action, you have to be very careful about where the action is coming from. The action comes from the actor.

Why do we have to be mindful of the actor rather than the action? Because we are that actor, and it is the actor that feels and suffers. The action is just a manifestation of the actor. The actor is the real thing. Why is the actor the real thing? Because all this discussion is for the sake of the actor. I am the actor, you are the actor. The actor wants to understand; the actor is restless. The action is not restless. Action, in that sense, is an insentient, inanimate thing. Actions have no sentience, no consciousness. The actor is sentient; the actor has consciousness; the actor, we said, suffers. And because it is the actor that suffers, all the emphasis has to be on knowing the actor. Looking at actions is obviously important, but not in order to know the action itself. You are looking at the action to know the actor.

Looking at action and getting involved with assessment of the action will not take you very far. Action can be deceptive:

to hide himself or to project a particular kind of image, the actor can indulge in deceptive action. We experience that every day, don't we? Somebody comes with a very broad grin on his face. The grin, the smile is the action. But that action is deceptive. You know very well that the person is not really joyful from inside. He is smiling at you, but he does not even really wish you well.

Therefore, action, though insignificant in itself, is yet an important means to come to the actor.

The moot point remains this: You must know who you are.

We are the ego-self, and the ego-self feels incomplete all the time, and, therefore, it is mandatory for it to indulge in action. How can it rest? It cannot rest feeling incomplete, insufficient, problemed all the time. Therefore, it continuously keeps acting. Therefore, the ego is the actor. And since we are the ego, to know ourselves is to know the doer. There is no way to know ourselves except by knowing the doer.

The doer is an invisible entity. How will you detect the doer? You cannot look at the doer with your eyes. All that you can look at with your eyes is the doing. Therefore, the doing is important. Therefore, you must look at the action.

You must look at the action and that makes action important, but action is important only because it will lead you to the actor. Otherwise, action by itself holds little value.

Looking at actions is obviously important, but not in order to know the action itself. You are looking at the action to know the actor.

20

The Actor Is the Action

Advait Shivir, Rishikesh, 2018

By condemning the doing and condoning the doer, you
are just preserving the doer to continue with the doing.

~

Questioner (Q): I do not accept someone hurting someone else. Is it right to say, 'Do not reject the person, reject the action?'

Acharya Prashant (AP): Is it really possible to draw a line between the actor and the action? Is it possible to say that the action is being rejected but the actor is all right?

The action is nothing but a gross manifestation of the actor. The doing depends on the doer. You will do what you are.

By condemning the doing and condoning the doer, you are just preserving the doer to continue with the doing. The doing is immaterial. The doing was inevitable. Given what you are, what else could have you done? You had no option.

If something has to be addressed, it is not the doing but the doer. Pay attention to who is doing this. If he remains the same, the same kind of actions will continue to come from him.

Actions just don't drop from somewhere; they don't come from an isolated vacuum. They arise from your self-concept; they arise from your idea of who you are and what the world is like. If the idea remains the same, the action will repeat itself in other situations, in other names, in other ways.

So, forget the action. Look at the actor.

You talked of hurt. Who gets hurt? Who wants to preserve himself? If there is no desire of self-preservation, is hurt possible? If you do not want to continue with something, keep something safe, protect something, if you do not want to not alter something, not expose something, is it possible to still get hurt?

Look at the thing, the entity that gets hurt. What is it? Where there is hurt, there must be fear. If you are vulnerable towards hurt, you would want to not get hurt, and you would be afraid that you might get hurt.

Who gets hurt? Who is so weak and vulnerable?

Who is the one needing a defense, an armour?

Who is the one forever doubtful of his strength?

Who is the one who knows deep down that he will crumble under pressure?

Who is the one who knows that he is bound to be defeated when attacked?

Who is the one who knows that his days are numbered?

Who is the one who knows that he is not trustworthy? Who is that?

What within us is so insecure that it keeps getting hurt?

Please figure that out. Who is that?

Is it really a virtue to not hurt someone? That's conventional wisdom. That's traditional religiosity. I want you to look at the matter with insight rather than indebtedness to tradition.

Q: Those actions or feelings are a product of the programming which you had mentioned before. I am assuming they are not a representation of the true self.

AP: Yes, they are a part of the programming, and that is why they are so prone to get hurt. You mentioned true self. Does the true self get hurt? Ever?

Q: The programme is like a virus in this world. Can we cure this virus? Can we heal this virus? Or should we accept the virus as it is?

AP: Maybe that which you are calling as 'we' is another name for the virus. How would the virus heal itself? A computer virus becomes lethal when it is packaged as an antivirus. Then you pay to put the virus in your system.

You have talked of two entities: 'me' and the virus. This 'me' is trying to cure or get rid of the virus. Who is this 'me'? If he is a product of the virus, would he be able to do away with the virus? First of all, is it not important to see and ensure that the 'me' is not an outcome of the virus? Should that not be the first question? Is the 'me' true enough, pure enough, healthy enough? If you are healthy enough, then maybe you can identify and isolate the virus, or do something or not do something. Health comes first, then we will see.

One has to see where one's actions are coming from because there is no other way to have self-knowledge. The virus is not a physical thing; you can never hold it in your hand, can you? It is a concept, an abstraction. It can be known only through its deeds, through its tangible manifestations.

The virus is known only by the effect it has upon you, and that effect is obvious in your daily actions, minute-to-minute life. Observe that, see that, and then you will be able to figure out whether there is actually some virus lurking behind your daily life.

Q: So, if this virus is a reflection of society, then there must be some positives in the so-called virus. What we have been told by society cannot be all bad.

AP: We are born with a virus. That which is born is a virus.

You talked of positives. Yes, that which society gives you can be positive, but only in the sense that the social input must heal you of the virus that you were born with. The child is born, the child is already infested, so what do you give the child? Particular medicine and injections. You understand 'injecting'? You are putting something into the child's system from outside; it is called 'injecting'.

Now, why are you giving all these injections to the child? So that he might be cured of the virus he was born with. That is the only positive possible. If there are people or institutions in society who give you inputs that dissolve your pre-existing tendencies, that is the only thing that you can call as positive.

So, there is no real positive, positive in the sense of addition. The injection does not really add to the child; the injection rather takes something away from the child's system. What does the injection take away? The only positive is to not add something but rather deduct something, reduce something. If you want to still use the word 'positive' for it, it is all right, but 'positive' is not really an exact word for the spiritual process.

(*A stone tumbles down the mountain in the distance*) You heard that rumbling? The stone was sitting on the edge. All it needed was a gentle push. So, speak! Just one word can cause so much rumbling. One answer can cause the stone to leave its painful heights and descend into the Ganges.

Actions just don't drop from somewhere; they don't come from an isolated vacuum. They arise from your self-concept; they arise from your idea of who you are and what the world is like. If the idea remains the same, the action will repeat itself in other situations, in other names, in other ways.

21

The Gap between Understanding and Action

Advait Shivir, Bhopal, 2018

No expression can be a substitute to action. Even the most beautiful kind of expression is no substitute to right action. You could say that the right action is the only right expression.

~

'Every thought I have imprisoned in expression I must free by my deeds.'

—Kahlil Gibran

Questioner (Q): What are deeds? What is honest doing? What does Kahlil Gibran mean here?

Acharya Prashant (AP): In honest doing, realization guides thoughts, determination, and then that determination instantaneously turns into action. The doer is realization. The real doer is a certain clarity. And because there is clarity, there is a smooth flow: one doesn't have to stumble and ponder and consider and reconsider. What begins quickly reaches the end like a forceful stream. Streams with lesser force get lost in deserts, quagmires, and have to face all kinds of angles, bends, distributions.

Realization and action must go together, realization being the beginning and action being the end.

In between realization and action, there is the possibility of much happening, much consuming away of the momentum. All that which happens between realization and action is nothing but an internal ploy to prevent the circle from gaining completion, to prevent the stream from reaching the sea. And obviously, all that in-between-ness is possible only if realization is not complete.

Kahlil Gibran is saying, 'Every thought I have imprisoned in expression I must free by my deeds.'

No expression can be a substitute to action. Even the most beautiful kind of expression is no substitute to right action. You could say that the right action is the only right expression. Understanding expresses itself through action, understanding knows no other expression. Words are a very poor substitute for the right action. That is what Gibran is talking of here. He says that which is understood craves for its final expression as action in life.

The poet often lets his understanding become his words. To that extent, there is a flow. But if the words remain mere words and do not turn into life, then there is no freedom yet; the imprisonment continues.

It is not at all sufficient to talk of the Truth; one has to live the Truth. The Truth must sit not merely on your tongue but in all parts of your body. Your hands, your legs, your eyes, your ears must express it, not merely your tongue or your pen.

In fact, the frustration of the one who gives only half an expression is greater than the frustration of the one who gives very little expression. Therefore, often poets are very sad people. The ordinary man has very little clarity, and, therefore, very little responsibility to express his clarity. But poets have far greater clarity, and consequently far greater responsibility as well.

When the poet is not able to live what he has known, then his punishment is severe. He enjoys a certain bliss as well: that bliss is when he is able to write, compose, sing. But having known that bliss, he gets even more thirsty for complete joy, total freedom, effulgent ecstasy, and if that ecstasy doesn't come, he faces hell.

You must understand this very clearly. Those who have very little realization will also have very little suffering. This is quite strange because usually we think that lack of understanding causes suffering. That must be put in context.

If you have absolutely no understanding, you will have absolutely no suffering also. Suffering begins with awakening, and that is why often awakening is avoided because total sleep, deeply unconscious sleep, is also a state of no suffering. As you start waking up, you start experiencing pain. In total understanding, again there is no suffering. There is no suffering in zero understanding, and there is no suffering in total understanding, but there is a lot of suffering in between. It is that suffering that Kahlil Gibran is talking of.

As you listen to me, you are not someone with zero clarity. You already are awake, and, therefore, you already are in pain. There are only two ways left to remove that pain: either go back to your primitive sleep, or move towards total awakening with determination.

The one who has not seen the Truth will also not miss it. But once you have had a glimpse of its beauty, the sheer magnificence and splendor of the Truth, then to bear its absence is excruciating. Those who have not known any exalted states will be content with living in their ditches, but the ones who have had soaring flights will find it humiliating to again belong to the mud.

Kahlil Gibran's own life is a case in point. His compositions tell of both euphoric joy and deep melancholy, the reason being that his life would often not match his words. So, that which you have just quoted from Gibran is probably his own life experience.

Anything short of total expression, anything short of life itself devoted to the Truth—not merely a part of life, not merely an hour of the day—will keep the seeker in pain. And as the Truth will keep getting clearer, the pain will keep getting unbearable. Truth will, like a petulant child, keep asking the question: 'If you love me, why don't you dance with me?' Truth will, like an innocent beloved, keep asking the question: 'If you love me, why don't you live with me?'

Live what you love. Otherwise, the punishment is tremendous. Or if you are not prepared to drop your fears, then stop loving. Stop knowing. Give up all clarity. Take a U-turn if you can.

When you first come to know of that unspeakable beauty, when the ineffable first reveals itself to you, then it is wonderful to sing of it; then it is wonderful to run crazy, run amok talking of it, shouting of it. But after a point, just talking of it is not beautiful, rather disgraceful.

You must know when you have crossed over from the beautiful to the disgraceful. Initially, if you just compose hymns in praise of the divine beauty, it means you are on the right path; you are saying all the right things. But if you just keep saying all the right things, it means you are your own block in the path.

One may begin with words. But if one remains at words, then one is guilty of deliberate infidelity.

Those who have not known any exalted states will be content with living in their ditches, but the ones who have had soaring flights will find it humiliating to again belong to the mud.

22

Why Doesn't the Law of Karma Apply to Animals?

Advait Shivir, Bhopal, 2018

A dog is born a dog, lives as a dog, dies as a dog, and no dog lives in a state of consciousness that is very different from that of another dog.

~

Questioner (Q): Why doesn't the law of karma apply to animals?

Acharya Prashant (AP): It is said that human beings get bad results and punishment if they commit bad actions, but nothing of this sort is said about animals. The law of karma does not apply to animals because animals do not really have a choice in their actions. When there is no choice, there is no question of reward or punishment.

Human beings are in a peculiar situation. They can choose to side with their animalistic conditioning, or they can choose something higher—they can choose freedom, joy, love, liberation, compassion. Therefore, humans have a responsibility.

Animals don't have that responsibility. Animals are dictated fully by their biological conditioning. If there is an accident on the road outside, you do not really expect the street dogs to rescue and help the victims of the accident, do you? They are not supposed to. You will not get angry at the dogs when they do not come to help the injured ones.

A couple of motorcycle riders have met with an accident accident, they are lying on the road, and there are birds on the trees and dogs roaming about. They will not take any special interest. There are so many insects around, aren't there? Some snake is there in the bush, right? They do not really care for these two creatures who are lying, bleeding on the road. They do not care, and they will not attract any punishment because they are not supposed to. They just do not have the option to act in compassion.

No animal can be compassionate, really, because an animal is completely just *Prakriti*. The animal does not really have the option to have a liberated consciousness. The animal's consciousness is completely dominated by its physical conditioning. Therefore, the animal gets neither reward nor punishment, which is comfortable in a sense because the animal lives in a secure zone. A dog is born a dog, lives as a dog, dies as a dog, and no dog lives in a state of consciousness that is very different from that of another dog. You cannot say one dog is liberated and the other dog is not. You cannot say one dog is joyful and compassionate and the other dog is not. Dogs can have varying external situations, but internally all dogs are just dogs.

This is not the case with human beings. Human beings can vary greatly in their internal state: one human being can be full of compassion, and the other one can be spiteful, angry, vicious, and violent. Therefore, the one who is compassionate is rewarded; he made the right choice. The one who is vicious is punished by his viciousness itself; he made the wrong choice.

There is this great difference between animals and human beings, which also means that human beings must never justify their actions by taking examples of animals. For example, if you eat animal flesh, you cannot justify it by saying that a lion or a wolf also kills other animals to eat. A lion or a wolf has no option to not kill. You have that option. Man is not necessarily a herbivore; man is more of an omnivore. Therefore, that option is there. You could have decided to not kill but you chose in favour of killing, therefore you will be punished. The lion is never punished because the lion had no option; the lion has done nothing wrong. In fact, even if a lion kills a human being, it has not committed a crime—because that's how lions are, they are supposed to kill to eat. But if a man needlessly kills an animal, then the man will be punished, if not by law, then by existence.

So, that is a human being in the clearest terms. A human being is a decision-maker; a human being is someone who has a choice. How do you define a human being? He is someone who has a choice. How you exercise these choices decides your life. Choose very, very carefully.

Human beings are in a peculiar situation. They can choose to side with their animalistic conditioning, or they can choose something higher—they can choose freedom, joy, love, liberation, compassion.

23

If One Is Brahman, Why Does One Work?

Advait Shivir, Bhopal, 2018

You aren't happy with yourself, and the proof is that you want to change and improve, don't you? And still you want to follow your own whims and desires. Isn't that stupid?

~

Questioner (Q): If I keep remembering that I am *Brahman*, then why should I work?

Acharya Prashant (AP): Then you won't work, *Brahman* would work.

If you do not know that you are *Brahman*, then *you* work, and you work in your own little and illusioned ways.

When you know that 'you' are not, only *Brahman* is, then *Brahman* works—and *Brahman* works a lot without breaking a sweat.

Look at the entire universe; there is so much happening. Who is the worker? Do you know how much work it takes to keep a planet in its orbit? You want to launch a little satellite into space, and you keep crying about fuel: the engines are not yet ready, the fuel is not compatible—and what are you trying to deliver into orbit? Just a little satellite! And here you have millions of planets and suns and stars, all fully established. And black holes and supernovas.

Who is working so hard? Who is working so beautifully?

You cannot run one nuclear reactor properly—there are accidents—and you think of a million safeguards. Have you looked at the nuclear reactor that gives you light every day? Who is running that nuclear reactor? He runs it without a blemish. And it is a very small sample of all the nuclear reactors that He runs.

Let something beyond you work through you. You will be amazed; you will be thrilled. You will then know what it means to really live.

If you are living only for yourself, if you are so afraid that you cannot give up your control of yourself, then all you get is 'yourself'.

Are you happy with yourself? Are you somebody whose company you would enjoy? If you have only yourself to talk to, would you prefer that? No. The proof is that you keep looking for others to talk to. You aren't happy with yourself, and the proof is that you want to change and improve, don't you? And still you want to follow your own whims and desires. Isn't that stupid?

If you are so established and arrived and wise, then why do you want to change? But you want to change all the time, don't you? 'How do I become better?' That's the question you are always asking, which means that you accept that as you are, you are not quite all right. If you are not quite all right, why do you chase directions dictated by your own desires?

Let something beyond you work through you. You will be amazed; you will be thrilled. You will then know what it means to really live.

24

Karma or Coincidence?

With IIT Kharagpur, 2020

Things are things, situations are situations, events are
events, external stimuli are just external. You have
no control over them. But, potentially, you have all
possible control over the one within who responds to
external situations. That is where your authority lies.

~

Questioner (Q): When something good or bad happens
unexpectedly to someone, is it karma or mere coincidence?

Acharya Prashant (AP): The happening is just a random
coincidence. How you experience the happening is your own
decision, your own doing, in other words, karma.

Get the difference right. The material world is not
predetermined. It is not even deterministic; it is random in
the real sense of the word. There are just too many cause
and effect nodes to take care of, and additionally there is the
unpredictable element of free will involved with respect to
many of the actors.

If the entire material world were a colossal machine, we
could have said that a day will come when we will be able
to fully map the machine, and if we can know the machine
fully, then we can determine, predict all that would happen in
the machine at a particular time and place. Then everything
becomes predictable.

But the machine is not only gigantic, several parts of it also carry free will, so unexpected things happen. Therefore, you cannot really know what is going to happen next in the external world. It is going to be a coincidence.

Kindly do not think that things are predetermined or that certain things are happening to you because you are destined to experience them. No, nothing of that kind. Fatalism is a sham.

The external world is truly unpredictable. Having said that, how you respond to what happens to you is very much your own decision, and there you have all the authority, all the ownership, and a lot of possible freedom.

So, things happen. Whether they are good or bad depends on your response and inner constitution. Where does your inner constitution come from? Your inner constitution is not really random because you are a conscious being: you have freedom in deciding what you must be, and you have freedom in building yourself up.

The one who responds to an experience from within is not a random occurrence. The one who responds to an external stimulus is the result of your entire life journey.

The same thing can happen to two people and they might respond very differently. Why is that so? The external event is the same. Something inside them must be different. From where does this thing inside come from? It comes from the accumulated set of your choices, and that is what is called karma in popular parlance.

You have brought yourself to a stage where you will respond negatively or favourably to an incident, where an incident will impact you greatly or not at all. That is *your* doing. That is what *you* have done.

So, it is not that good things are happening to you or bad things are happening to you. Things are things, situations are situations, events are events, external stimuli are just external. You have no control over them. But, potentially, you have all possible control over the one within, who responds to external situations. That is where your authority lies. That is what you can control. That is what you must have all power over. That is the entire purpose of life, and that is freedom. Otherwise, you are just a slave of situations: situations can come and drive you mad. That is no way to live.

So, good and bad things that happen, are they karma—in other words, a result of our past actions, deeds, choices, etc.—or coincidence?

Both.

To what extent are these things coincidental? To the extent they are external. The external world, we said, is random. Anything can happen to anybody anytime. There is no guarantee of any fixed thing happening. Things are probabilistic at best.

But when it comes to the inner world, how you respond to what happens to you is your choice, your decision, and that decision cannot be taken fully in this moment itself because it is a thing that accumulates.

You have to build yourself up rightly. You cannot say you want to remain uninfluenced by all the catastrophic situations outside and wish that what you want just happens.

If you really want to be uninfluenced by the external situations, you will have to work very hard at developing that kind of a core within. That is karma.

25

What Is Hard Work in Spiritual Terms?

Advait Shivir, BodhSthal, 2019

In life, it is not the number of calories that you have burnt that matter so much; rather it is the purpose for which you are burning those calories.

~

'By his non-action the sage governs all.'

—Lao Tzu

'Non-action is unceasing activity. The sage is characterized by eternal and intense activity.'

—Ramana Maharshi

Acharya Prashant (AP): Man can either have no false centre or a billion false centres. The animal will necessarily have one false centre: the name of that false centre is *Prakriti* (physical nature). Man can either have no false centre, or man can have innumerable false centres. Lao Tzu and Ramana Maharshi here are talking about someone who has no false centre.

Questioner (Q): Compared to the sage, I find myself not only lacking in motivation but also in the capacity to work hard, to indulge in intense activity. Can the capacity to work hard be developed at an older age?

AP: You don't have to develop the capacity to work hard. You have to allow the right and appropriate work to happen. The sage does not work hard; he allows the right work to happen through him. Maharshi says, 'Intense unceasing activity.' Kindly do not draw conclusions. Kindly do not imagine that the Maharshi or Lao Tzu is talking about hard work. They are not talking in terms of the number of calories burnt; they are talking in terms of intensity.

Intensity in work is a description of the extent to which your work is emanating from an intensely deep place within you. That is what is meant by intensity of work. I repeat, intensity of work does not refer to the number of calories burnt.

Intensity of the work refers to the depth of the point, the intensity of the point, from where the work is arising.

There might be a lot of intensity involved in just saying yes. This is intense work. And there might be no intensity at all involved in a decade of soul-sapping hard work. There is no dearth of hard workers in the world. But do they have intensity? No. To be intense is to work from the right centre; it does not relate to anything else. It is quite possible that over an entire decade you have just been saying no; that is the sum total of your entire work. What did you do the entire decade? 'I said no.' But then, it could still be very, very intense and unceasing work.

Therefore, it is not about your body or this or that. We are not talking about the gym here, nor are we talking about breaking stones or running a marathon. We are talking about life. In life, it is not the number of calories that you have burnt that matter so much; rather it is the purpose for which you are burning those calories. And remember, the purpose of work is exactly the same as the centre of the work; where you are coming from will be exactly the same as where you are going to.

So, neither Lao Tzu nor Ramana Maharshi is encouraging the disciples to run around and show some hard work in the same sense as military people or sports persons do. They are talking about right work. And right work is very hard to do. Therefore, right work is the real hard work. There is a lot of hard work that is not right work but is chosen simply because it is easy. Therefore, that hard work is not hard work, but cheap, easy, compromised work.

Never honour somebody purely on the basis of the number of hours of work they have put in, or the calories they have burnt, or the number of units they have manufactured, or the amounts they have earned. That is not the real or spiritual way of looking at things. If you really have to assess somebody's work, assess the work by its centre. Where is the work coming from? Which direction is it going towards?

We very well know that it is easier—often far easier— to spend a decade running around than to spend an hour standing still. Now you know what hard work really is. I am not favouring standing still over running around; I am just trying to correct your notions, your perceptions. I am not offering you an alternate perception. When I say that it is possible that you might have worked very diligently for ten years and yet your hard work is not hard work but cheap work, by that I do not mean to encourage all the loafers and lazy people.

Right work could mean anything: sometimes it could mean standing still, sometimes it could mean a lot of physical activities. Standing still does not matter, abundance of physical activities does not matter; the only thing that matters is where the thing, be it stillness or movement, is coming from.

You have talked of your physical capacity and age. Look at a river or look at a tree. Both have a life cycle. Once the tree was tender and young; there was a particular way it responded to the wind. Now the tree is getting old; now there is another way it responds to the wind. Both are beautiful. You don't have to emulate somebody else; you just have to avoid resisting the wind.

Please get the difference. The older tree does not have to say that 'I must still be supple and flexible and dance like the younger tree'. It cannot do that. It is now physically incapable of doing that. It has grown old, there is a lot of bark, it is not so tender and flexible anymore. If it tries to bend too much and dance around, probably it will break. But it can still love the wind and offer no resistance to it.

That is the sage. He offers no resistance to the wind. In the case of the tree, the wind is outside. In case of the sage, the wind is inside. The situation of the sage is one of non-resistance. 'I do not resist the wind, but that does not mean that I will deliberately and forcibly dance to the wind. Let the wind do what it can. Who am I? I am nobody. I do not have a centre. So, I leave it to the wind. Let the wind decide what it wants to do with me. If I decide not to dance to the wind, that is true worship. And if I decide to forcibly dance to the wind, that, too, is true worship. There was a time when I could dance a lot to the wind—I was not the doer; the wind was the doer. And now I cannot dance so much to the wind—even now I am not the doer, the wind is. One day the wind will probably uproot me, I am getting old—even then I will not be the doer, the wind will be the doer.'

Such is the condition of the sage. When the body of the sage is young, it dances to the inner centre in one way; when the body is older, it dances in another way. The sage does not bother. The body is not his. Why must he bother? Why must he push the body? To display an exaggerated dance? No.

The inner centre owns the body. Let the inner centre manage its own domestic affairs. The body is the affair of the inner centre. Who is the sage to intervene? The sage says, 'I am nobody. The body belongs to you. If you can make the body do this much (*gestures indicating small movement*), or if you can make the body do this much (*gestures indicating large movement*), proceed. I would neither resist nor cooperate. My task is to just not resist. My task is to be absent. Who am I to interfere? You decide. Thy will be done. You know my body, you know my legs, you know my age. I am your servant; I have no personal will. I do not exist. I am not the actor. I am merely a servant. I have surrendered to that extent. You are the master. You know everything about me. If you still order me to run along to the market, I will do that. I will honour your wish if that is what you want, because you know best. I do not know. Looking at my age, looking at my knees, looking at my lungs, if you still feel that I need to run to the market, I will honour your wish, I will not question you. I will not even express happiness.'

This is the condition of the sage. He takes no personal responsibility for himself. He has given himself away to the real Self. 'Thy will be done. You are the master.'

Unconditional obedience, total surrender, and, therefore, intense action—not necessarily hard work.

Right work could mean anything: sometimes it could mean standing still, sometimes it could mean a lot of physical activities. Standing still does not matter, abundance of physical activities does not matter; the only thing that matters is where the thing, be it stillness or movement, is coming from.

26

Past-Life Karma, Goal of Life, and Liberation

Advait Shivir, Hyderabad, 2019

'Eternity' and 'continuity' are words only for those who do not live in the personality. If you live in the personality, you need not wait even for your physical death: you are dying continuously.

~

Questioner (Q): Do you believe in past lives?

Acharya Prashant (AP): That is irrelevant. Will I find you after your death? Will even you find yourself after your death?

Q: I might be in a different body.

AP: In a different body, will you have the same psyche, the same identity? You are a person, and a person is driven by identities. Forget about having a new life after death; even in this life, if I give you the option that your personality will be totally wiped out—your memory will be totally wiped out, your body will be totally changed, and you will be taken to a different place, a different planet—will you still say that you are 'you'? Will you still say that?

Even in this life, if your memory gets wiped out, do you remain what you are? Even in this life, if somebody strikes your head with a hammer and your memory is totally gone— which means your identities are totally gone—you are as good as dead, you are of no use to anybody; you do not remain. You have disappeared because you are a man of identities, because you are a personality. You live in a personality, and once the personality is gone, once the person is gone, you are no more.

'Eternity' and 'continuity' are words only for those who do not live in the personality.

If you live in the personality, you need not wait even for your physical death: you are dying continuously. Even tomorrow you will not be who you are today. Then how will you continue to be the same in your next birth? Even today you are not what you were fifteen years back, are you? Then how will you continue to remain two hundred years from today? But it is such a stupid thought—still, very common.

Do you feel one or identify with the self that you were when you were ten years of age? Go into this. You, as you see yourself, were once ten years of age, right? Today, do you find much in common with that ten-year-old kid? In fact, today, 90 per cent of you is not common with that ten-year-old kid, right? In the same lifetime, you are almost a totally different person, are you not? Then how will you remain the same after death even if there is a rebirth? So, what is the point in talking about this and that?

Q: So, thirtieth birthday means thirty years of death?
AP: Yes, nice. Good.

Q: We said that memories being wiped out is equivalent to the person not being there. Now, this is a bit confusing, as we just talked about us not being the body.
AP: But are you the Ātman? I said that 'eternity' and 'continuity' are words applicable only to those who live as the

Ātman. Do you live as the Ātman? If you live as the Ātman, then you will not talk of this birth and the previous birth because the Ātman never really dies. So, how can it take the next birth? To take the next birth, something must die. Ātman is eternal, it does not die. How can it take a new birth?

Q: Many religions, like Hinduism and Jainism, talk of past lives and rebirth. It seems that you do not want to be consistent with them.
AP: What do you want?

Q: I just want . . .
AP: Those who 'just want' anything do not get anything. Talk of one thing that you want and then don't talk of anything else.

Q: I want the Truth.
AP: Yes.

Truth is freedom from the false. See what all is false in the way you currently live.

Two things: 'currently' and 'living'. Go into your life, right now.

How do you spend your day?

Where do you eat?

Where do you earn your money from?

These are the questions that should bother you, not fancy intellectual questions.

Q: The worldly matters, what I do and all that, is that a part of spirituality?
AP: What do you want to do with 'spirituality' and 'worldly matters'? The one who is in trouble wants freedom from

trouble. If the name of that freedom is 'spirituality', fine. If the name of that freedom is 'worldliness', fine. What the person wants is freedom. If I am thirsty, I want water. If you want to call it *jal, ambu, waari* (synonyms for water in Hindi), anything, I do not mind. Give me that which will quench my thirst. Full stop.

Q: I have a question related to thoughts and concentration. If thoughts can increase the level of concentration, how can we make them do so?
AP: Goal.

Q: How to magnify and amplify that goal?
AP: In the example that you gave when we were playing football, you mentioned that there was a clear distinction, that each team knew where their goal post is. In real life there are ten goal posts being shown, and each one is trying to instruct that this is where you have to reach. Unfortunately, sometimes the goal posts look similar, and one gets confused.

   Who is suffering?

Q: I am suffering.
AP: So, who will know whether or not you are getting freedom?
   (Silence)
   Who is suffering?
   (Silence)
   It is like this: I am thirsty. One guru tells me to put water in this hole *(points to the ear)*, another guru tells me to put water in this hole *(points to the mouth)*, another one talks about the other holes of the body.

Who is thirsty? You are. Don't you know when your thirst is quenched? Why are you acting so ignorant? Don't you know your own thirst, your own suffering? Don't you know when it is being quenched?

Q: I have not even reached the point where my thirst is being quenched.

AP: At least you know when it is not being quenched. This much at least you know.

Q: Yes.

AP: Next time, don't put water in your ear. Reject the guru who teaches you to put water in your ear. At least this much you can do. Do this much.

Q: But the problem is that when one is thirsty, it is water that one needs. When one gets a cool drink nearby, one is tempted to take it.

AP: Try it, immediately. You are already thirty or forty years old, or maybe twenty-five. How many more trials do you need? Have you already not given everything a shot? Are soft-drinks or ice creams or petroleum new things to you? You have already tried them a thousand times. Are you still not fed up?

If you are not fed up, give them one more chance, and then be absolutely fed up.

But please, at some point, learn to be honest, learn to quit. Learn to honestly face the mirror and tell yourself, 'I have been cheating myself all my life.'

If you don't do that, there are a thousand kinds of fluids in the universe. You will keep trying them endlessly.

Water is simple water—pure, direct. I have no issues if you want to give various things, various methods, various means, various books, various teachers a chance. Please do that. But do that with all honesty. Having given the chance, ask yourself, 'Is the thirst being quenched?' If yes, then stay put, then don't budge at all. If no, then you have no business looking at that face ever again.

Man is a strange creature. He develops a stake even in thirst. If you have conditioned yourself to find pleasure in thirst, in suffering, in nonsense, then . . .

Q: What is the significance of sleep? What really happens in sleep? What is the spiritual significance of sleep?

AP: Are your problems in your sleep time, or are your problems related to your waking state? Don't be interested in miscellaneous knowledge, focus on the goal. Any kind of knowledge that does not lead you directly towards the goal is merely a burden. Disregard it.

If you have genuine problems, sleeping disorders, then talk to me about sleep. But if your problems are related to your life, stuff that you think of in your waking state—your relationships, your transactions—then why be interested in sleep? I can speak for fifteen minutes on sleep, but that will not help you.

Be direct, be honest.

Q: Why is my mind constantly trying to become something?

AP: Everybody is trying that because nobody is content with the current state. The only problem is: you want to change, but you want the changed state to be a derivative of the current state; you want the changed state to be organically linked to your current state, which means that you really don't want to give up your current state.

So, all becoming fails. All change is defeated. It is like changing clothes: that will not cure you of your lung cancer. It is like wearing makeup: that will not fundamentally cure your skin disorder. Change is wonderful. When you want change, see what you really want.

But don't change half-heartedly. Change fully.

If you are not fed up, give them one more chance, and then be absolutely fed up. But please, at some point, learn to be honest, learn to quit. Learn to honestly face the mirror and tell yourself, 'I have been cheating myself all my life.'

PART IV

WHAT DO THE SCRIPTURES SAY?

27

The Secret of Right Action

Gita Samagam, BodhSthal, 2020

Sacrificing is a very wise trade-off; it is a bargain in wisdom. You're giving up something that has a lower value, and having given this thing up, you attain something that has a higher value. This is yagya.

~

दैवमेवापरे यज्ञं योगिनः पर्युपासते ।
ब्रह्माग्नावपरे यज्ञं यज्ञेनैवोपजुह्वति ॥

श्रोत्रादीनीन्द्रियाण्यन्ये संयमाग्निषु जुह्वति ।
शब्दादीन्विषयानन्य इन्द्रियाग्निषु जुह्वति ॥

सर्वाणीन्द्रियकर्माणि प्राणकर्माणि चापरे ।
आत्मसंयमयोगाग्नौ जुह्वति ज्ञानदीपिते ॥

द्रव्ययज्ञास्तपोयज्ञा योगयज्ञास्तथापरे ।
स्वाध्यायज्ञानयज्ञाश्च यतयः संशितव्रताः ॥

अपाने जुह्वति प्राणं प्राणेऽपानं तथापरे ।
प्राणापानगती रुद्ध्वा प्राणायामपरायणाः ॥

अपरे नियताहाराः प्राणान्प्राणेषु जुह्वति ।
सर्वेऽप्येते यज्ञविदो यज्ञक्षपितकल्मषाः ॥

यज्ञशिष्टामृतभुजो यान्ति ब्रह्म सनातनम् ।
नायं लोकोऽस्त्ययज्ञस्य कुतोऽन्यः कुरुसत्तम ॥

एवं बहुविधा यज्ञा वितता ब्रह्मणो मुखे ।
कर्मजान्विद्धि तान्सर्वानेवं ज्ञात्वा विमोक्ष्यसे ॥

श्रेयान्द्रव्यमयाद्यज्ञाज्ज्ञानयज्ञः परन्तप ।
सर्वं कर्माखिलं पार्थ ज्ञाने परिसमाप्यते ॥

*Other yogis undertake sacrifice to gods alone, others
offer the self, as a sacrifice by the self itself, in the fire
of Brahman.*

*Others offer the organs, viz. ear etc., in the fires of self-
control. Others offer the objects, viz. sound etc., in the
fires of the organs.*

*Others offer all the activities of the organs and the
activities of the vital force into the fire of the yoga of
self-control which has been lighted by Knowledge.*

*Similarly, others are performers of sacrifices through
wealth, through austerity, through yoga, and through
study and knowledge; others are ascetics with severe
vows.*

*Constantly practising control of the vital forces by
stopping the movements of the outgoing and the
incoming breaths, some offer as a sacrifice the outgoing
breath in the incoming breath; while still others, the
incoming breath in the outgoing breath.*

Others, having their food regulated, offer the vital forces in the vital forces. All of them are knowers of the sacrifice and have their sins destroyed by sacrifice.

Those who partake of the nectar left over after a sacrifice, reach the eternal Brahman. This world ceases to exist for one who does not perform sacrifices. What to speak of the other (world), O best among the Kurus!

Thus, various kinds of sacrifices lie spread at the mouth of the Vedas. Know them all to be born of action. Knowing thus, you will become liberated.

O destroyer of enemies, Knowledge considered as a sacrifice is greater than sacrifices requiring materials. O son of Pārtha, all actions in their totality culminate in knowledge.

—Shrimad Bhagavad Gita,
Chapter 4, Verses 25 to 33

~

Questioner (Q): From verse 25 to 33 of chapter 4, Shri Krishna speaks of the following sacrifices to gods: sacrifice of self, which is the ego, *aham*; sacrifice of organs of senses; sacrifice of objects of senses; sacrifice of functions of senses; sacrifice of wealth; sacrifice by austerities; sacrifice by study of scriptures; sacrifice by restraint of breath; and sacrifice of diet.

What is really meant by sacrifice or *yagya*, and what is really meant by *jñāna-yagya* that Krishna calls as greater than all the other sacrifices or *yagya*?

Also, please help us understand the meaning of verse 33 that says, 'All actions in their totality culminate in knowledge.'
Acharya Prashant (AP): No, no. That is not what verse 33 says. Not 'culminate' in knowledge; *dissolve* in knowledge. The word used is *'parisamāpyate'*; an ending, *samapti*. The word *'apti'* means highest, a climax. *Samapti* means having truly attained the climax. That is *samapti*.

So, when it is said here that all actions in their totality culminate in knowledge, what is meant is that real understanding gives you a dissolution of all actions; all actions dissolve in understanding. What does that mean? What is it that actions leave behind?

Q: Their consequences.
AP: Their fruits, right? Their residues. But in understanding, actions do not leave behind any residue because you do not act for the sake of the residue; the action itself is chosen so wisely that it will not leave behind any fruit, any clutter, any dirt. It simply means *niṣkāma-karma*. You do not act for the sake of the result. That is the mark of wisdom or understanding. You just act; therefore, action leaves you with no obligations, no achievements, nor any heartbreaks.

What is an achievement? What is a feeling of elation? What is this euphoria on the success of an action? It is the fruit of action, right? I acted, and my action achieved the target it was directed at, so now I am feeling elated. This is a residue of action. The action has left me with elation; elation is a residue of the action.

Similarly, what is disappointment or heartbreak? The action did not fetch me what I wanted from it, so what has the action left me with? Despair. Sadness. What is this sadness? It is a residue or fruit of the action.

Both of these residues come only to those who act in order to get something. Get something for whom? For whom is the euphoria? To whom is the sadness?

Q: To oneself.

AP: To the actor. So, happiness or sadness come to you only when you act for the sake of your own gratification. When you do not act for the sake of your own personal benefit, then action leaves you with neither happiness nor sadness; you are free of the action. Your action has attained closure, fulfillment. That is what Krishna is saying here.

What if you are left with bitterness after the action? What will that lead to?

Q: Next action?

AP: Next action. So, you're not liberated. You're still under the obligation to act one more time because the action has left you with bitterness.

What if the action leaves you with a sense of accomplishment? Again, you will be tempted to act one more time. 'You see, I got something. Can't I repeat my success?' So, you're not liberated. You're not liberated because you are again obligated to . . .?

Q: Do the next action?

AP: Act one more time, and you have created future for yourself, so you're caught in the cycle of time. If you want to act one more time, what do you require? You require one more time; you require time. And if you require time, then you're still caught in the clockwork; you're not free of time; you're still in *Kalachakra* (the wheel of time). *Kāla* is time and *kāla* is death—and you will be afraid.

Now, the questioner is saying, 'What is meant by sacrifice and what is meant by *jñāna-yagya*, and why is *jñāna-yagya* higher than all other sacrifices?'

Sacrifice obviously means giving up or offering. At the root of sacrifice is realization. So, we will consider sacrifice, and we will consider what is *jñāna* or realization.

What is at the root of all sacrifice? When would you sacrifice something for something else?

Q: When I see that I would get something better.

AP: Seeing that the thing you have is of lower value than what you would get post . . .?

Q: Sacrificing.

AP: Sacrificing it. So, in that sense, it is actually just a trade-off. But it is a very wise trade-off; it is a bargain in wisdom. You're giving up something that has a lower value, and having given this thing up, you attain something that has a higher value. This is *yagya*.

Yagya says, 'Of what use is this little self to me? I give this up. Having given this self up, what do I get? I get the greater self, the real self, the pure self. I have given up the false self, the little self, the ego. Having given up the ego, I attain something immensely bigger.' So, it is a profitable bargain. A small thing has been given up, and something big has been attained.

Similarly, sacrifice of organs of senses, objects of senses, function of senses, wealth, this, that . . . Basically, we are talking of a value system here. We must know how to assess, how to evaluate. We must know what is the right value of one thing vis-à-vis another thing, and we must know that Truth and freedom are the most valuable; therefore, anything can be sacrificed for their sake. Hence, and then only, this becomes obvious, this thing falls in place. 'I can give up my wealth if giving up of wealth brings freedom to me. I can give up my knowledge; I can give up senses, pleasures, ego, concepts. All these things I can give up.'

And then some of the verses have also talked of the way of giving up. Three ways have been listed here by the questioner: sacrifice through austerity, sacrifice through study of scriptures, sacrifice through *prāṇayama* or restraint of breath. So, these are three ways of giving up. There is stuff that you give up, and there are ways in which you give up. What is central is the intention to give up. And remember that giving up in the spiritual sense is not charity; it is good business. You have given a smaller thing up and attained something . . .?

Q: Bigger.
AP: Far bigger. Infinitely more profitable. In fact, that is one way to define joy. Do not call joy as freedom from pleasure; just call joy as higher pleasure. Now, if you call joy as higher pleasure, then it becomes possible to sacrifice the lower pleasures for the sake of the higher pleasure called joy.

Otherwise, spirituality remains very scary to people who have been spoken to in the language of renunciation. 'Give this up, give that up.' The ego asks, 'But why? All I have is this 10-rupee note, and you're asking me to give it up!' You have to, in the same breath, tell him that by giving up this 10-rupee note, you will indeed get something that is worth Rs 500. And you have to really demonstrate it. He must be able to see it in his life that by giving up on smaller pleasures or the so-called good things of life, he has now attained a state that is far higher, a state that he would not like to exchange in return for anything.

When you do not act for the sake of your own personal benefit, then action leaves you with neither happiness nor sadness; you are free of the action. Your action has attained closure, fulfillment.

28

The Right Action for You Depends on Your Conditioning

Gita Samagam, BodhSthal, 2020

Dharma is the same for everybody, but swadharma varies according to your physical, social, temporal conditions. But remember that swadharma can never be in contradiction of Dharma; swadharma will always be something within the ambit of Dharma.

~

स्वधर्ममपि चावेक्ष्य न विकम्पितुमर्हसि ।
धर्म्याद्धि युद्धाच्छ्रेयोऽन्यत्क्षत्रियस्य न विद्यते ॥

Even considering your own duty you should not waver, since there is nothing else better for a Kshatriya than righteous battle.

—Shrimad Bhagavad Gita, Chapter 2, Verse 31

~

Questioner (Q): After explaining to Arjuna that he should not grieve for the embodied beings in verse 31 of the 2nd chapter of Bhagavad Gita, Shri Krishna says, 'Even considering your own duty you should not waver, since there is nothing else better for a Kshatriya than a righteous battle.'

Being born into a Kshatriya clan, fighting represents Arjuna's conditioning and training and what he has become good at. Does conditioning have a role in discovering one's duty or one's *swadharma*? Is adhering to one's *swadharma* the same as liberation?

Acharya Prashant (AP): You see, liberation is *Dharma*. To move to the point where one stands liberated alone is *Dharma*. But when we define *Dharma* this way, then we are talking of only one point: the point which you have to reach. We are calling that as the point of liberation.

Nobody stands at a position called 'no position', we all stand somewhere. Wherever we stand, that point is actually a point of conditioning. Had we not been standing somewhere, there was no need to travel to be liberated.

You could consider the point of liberation as the origin, (0,0). Think of basic x-y coordinates. So, liberation is at (0,0), the origin, and you have to go back to that very origin where everything comes from. But where are you currently located? You are located somewhere, you have some coordinates- (x,y). Or if you take three dimensions, then (x,y,z). How many various kinds of coordinates are possible? Infinite. The (x,y,z) combo can take infinite distinct values, correct?

Wherever you are currently located, from there you have to come to the origin. So, coming to the origin is *Dharma*, but *swadharma* is coming to the origin from where you are. Therefore, each person, each (x,y,z), will have his own particular path to come to the origin. That's why it is called *swadharma*, not just *Dharma*.

Swadharma means your *Dharma*. *Swadharma* is not really different from *Dharma*, but *Dharma* merely says, 'Come to the origin, come to zero. Come to the point where everything is dissolved, where nothing exists. Become zero.' *Swadharma* clarifies things a little more. *Swadharma* says, 'Yes, you have to come to zero, but you have to come from (4,5,8), (x,y,z).'

So, now things stand clearer: From (4,5,8) you have to come to zero, and now you can find out a route. Obviously, the shortest route is a straight line, but maybe the configurations, the situations stand in such a way that a straight line is not even possible, so you figure out some other route, whatever it is. The thing is that now you know that you have to move from (4,5,8) to (0,0,0).

Arjuna, too, stands somewhere. Had Arjuna not been standing somewhere, then Arjuna would have been standing at (0,0,0); then there would have been no need for any Krishna or any Gita as Arjuna is already at the origin. But where is Arjuna standing? Arjuna is standing where his body and the norms and situations and the customs and the conditioning of his time have made him stand. Krishna has to take that particular place into account, otherwise he would just be talking theory that would not be of much use to Arjuna.

So, Krishna not merely talks of liberation and freedom; he also keeps referring to Arjuna's Kshatriya clan. If you are really interested in covering a distance, you must know both the ends. Krishna must talk of the origin, (0,0,0), and Krishna must also equally, seriously talk of (4,5,8), which is Arjuna's configuration, coordinates at that point. That is why he repeatedly refers to Arjuna's Kshatriya caste.

Now, let's say, Krishna is talking to somebody belonging to the other *varnas*. He would be advising everybody, irrespective of whether he is a Kshatriya or a Vaishya or a Brahmin or a Shudra, to go to (0,0,0), but all would be advised to go to (0,0,0) starting from where they are actually and practically situated.

If you are standing at (4,5,8), you can't be told the same route that was told to someone who was standing at (2,3,11). If that route is suggested to you, you will never reach (0,0,0); you will fail, totally fail. So, now when he is talking to Arjuna, he is saying, 'You see, over the passage of time in the game of *Prakriti*, in the entire play of *Maya*, you have become a Kshatriya.'

Now, all that is just a superficial thing. The entire *varna* system has no depth; it is just a superficial arrangement made by man himself. But whatever it is, the thing is that it is taken as an identity statement by somebody like Arjuna—in fact, by all who were present at that time. They take their *varna*-identity as important.

Now, since they take it as important, Krishna tells them that according to your *varna*-identity—which is according to your present coordinates—this is how you should move to (0,0,0); you have to fight.

If a Brahmin is there on the same battlefield, Krishna would advise him to resist the Kauravas but in some way that is most suited to the Brahmin's own conditioning. If he tells the Brahmin to pick up the bow and arrow or mace and start fighting Duryodhana, then the war is lost already. So, the Brahmin will have to fight Duryodhana, no doubt, but in the way of the Brahmin. The Vaishya and the Shudra, too, will have to fight Duryodhana but in their own respective ways.

What is important is that when you reach (0,0,0), then the Kshatriya is no more a Kshatriya; he comes to learn that all this *varna* and caste thing is some kind of a man-made joke. But how will he learn that standing at (2,4,8)? Standing at (2,4,8), he is taking his caste very seriously. He says, 'I am a Kshatriya.' When will he be able to doubtlessly and convincingly say, 'I am not a Kshatriya—I am not even a body! How can I be a Kshatriya?' When will he be able to say that? Only when he reaches (0,0,0). But to reach (0,0,0), he has to start from being a Kshatriya.

So, even to come to the point where Arjuna is no more a Kshatriya, he has to start from a point where he indeed is a Kshatriya. In a way, Krishna is using the *varna* of Arjuna to bring him to a point where he is liberated from the *varna* system altogether. But even to liberate him of his class or caste or conditioning, he has to start from where he actually and practically is standing right now.

Krishna is doing something very wise and very practical at the same time. When you come to that origin point, differences cease to exist: There is no difference between a Brahmin, a Vaishya, a Shudra, a Kshatriya, anybody; there is no difference between a man and a woman; there is no difference at all. But in this world that we see all around us, first of all there are physical differences of age, of gender, of race, and then there are social differences: caste, creed, ethnicity, nationality, religion. We live in a world of differences.

Even to bring someone to a point where he would be liberated of differences, you have to see what his current configuration is. If you are not mindful of his current configuration, then your attempts to help him will fail— and Krishna is not someone who is going to fail. So, he repeatedly reminds Arjuna that he is a Kshatriya. His identity is repeatedly evoked: 'Arjuna, you are a Kshatriya, and the Kshatriya must fight.'

Now, both the things are at play here, *Dharma* and *swadharma*. In what does *Dharma* lie? *Dharma* lies in fighting Duryodhana. In what does *swadharma* lie? *Swadharma* lies in fighting Duryodhana like a Kshatriya.

Let's say, if a Brahmin was present at the battlefield, *Dharma* would remain the same for Arjuna and that Brahmin: *Dharma* is to fight Duryodhana because Duryodhana is representing *adharma*. But *swadharma* will be different: Arjuna's *swadharma* will be to fight Duryodhana like a warrior, and the Brahmin's *swadharma* will be to fight Duryodhana like a scholar.

So, *Dharma* is the same for everybody, but *swadharma* varies according to the kind of personality you have taken. According to your physical, social, temporal conditions, *swadharma* varies, but remember that *swadharma* can never be in contradiction of *Dharma*; *swadharma* will always be something within the ambit of *Dharma*.

Dharma is: fight Duryodhana. *Swadharma* is: fight Duryodhana with bows and arrows. Why with bows and arrows? 'Because Arjuna, that is all you can do. What else will you do? Over the last 45 years, Arjuna, if there is one thing that you have learnt—and there is only one thing that you have learnt—it is to fight. There is only one thing you have continuously practised, which is your bow and arrow. So, now that you have to fight Duryodhana, what other method or weapon do you have? You have only one excellence; there is only one thing that you know. There is only one way in which you can fight Duryodhana, which is your Kshatriya way, because there is no other way that you know. So, fight Duryodhana in your own way.' That is *swadharma*.

Fighting Duryodhana is *Dharma*. Fight Duryodhana in the way you can, that is *swadharma*.

अकीर्तिं चापि भूतानि कथयिष्यन्ति तेऽव्ययाम् ।
सम्भावितस्य चाकीर्तिर्मरणादतिरिच्यते ॥

People also will speak of your unending infamy. And to an honoured person infamy is worse than death.
—Shrimad Bhagavad Gita, Chapter 2, Verse 34

Q: In verse 34 of chapter 2, Shri Krishna says to Arjuna, 'People will also speak of your unending infamy, and to an honoured person infamy is worse than death.'

But at the time of King Dasharatha's death, Guru Vashishtha says, 'Loss-profit, life-death, glory-infamy, all are in the hands of destiny.'

The two contexts are different. In the first, a warrior is being urged to act, and the second is on the occasion of the death of a king. It makes me wonder about the connection of infamy with one's actions. Does a righteous action need to be influenced by how the world perceives it?

Also, when Krishna is urging Arjuna to remain equanimous in pleasure and pain and life and death, then why does he ask Arjuna to consider infamy as worse than death when such a consideration might disturb his equanimity?

AP: First of all, what is Shri Krishna doing?

On the battlefield, the forces of darkness have to be fought. If Duryodhana occupies power, it is not going to be good for Hastinapur and the adjoining states, probably the larger part of the entire subcontinent. At least all the states that come within the influence of Duryodhana's power will have to suffer.

Duryodhana has repeatedly displayed his proclivity towards injustice, corruption, fame, lustfulness, treachery, many kinds of evil. He is not at all an eligible candidate to occupy the throne, and that is the reason Shri Krishna is siding with the Pandavas. It is not about ensuring that one party gets its rightful claim on the throne; the issue is wider. It is about the entire population.

Remember that Mahabharata is not an age of democracy. The king used to have unlimited authority. He was supposed to be a representative of God, and all that he did or said had to be respected, obeyed. In such situations, the personal disposition of the king towards *Dharma*, towards justice, was very critical in determining the welfare or the disaster of an entire population. Give the population the right kind of king and you have one kind of result and give the population an evil king and you have a totally different, disastrous result.

So, the question of who the king will be was a very crucial question in determining the very fate of Bharata (India). Therefore, sides had to be taken. Therefore, Krishna had to really stand with and behind the Pandavas to ensure that they win. Therein lay *Dharma*: fight Duryodhana; he is the mascot of evil right now.

But who will fight Duryodhana? Arjuna. Is Arjuna a liberated person? No. Arjuna is very much a product of his time; Arjuna very much believes in his *varna* or caste-identity very strongly. Arjuna is someone who is quite strongly attached to his family members; familial bonds matter a lot to him. The Gita opens with the sight of Arjuna shivering and trembling and feverish and refusing to pick up the Gandiva because he cannot. He says he does not have enough power in his hands at the moment to even pick up his weapon. That is his state. Does it look like a state of some perfect person? No, not at all.

Over his entire lifetime, Arjuna had displayed normal human tendencies. Obviously, he was a good human being, he had to be. He had befriended Krishna, he tolerated a lot, he was often seen fighting for the right cause, defending the right kind of people. But still, he was more or less an ordinary mortal.

Now, such an ordinary mortal, let's say a little better than ordinary, such a person needs to be roped in to fight against Duryodhana. Merely telling him that fighting Duryodhana is important for the welfare of north India would be no good. Those kinds of *Dharmic* invocations would not matter so much to Arjuna.

Arjuna is riled in his own inner battles, attachments, old memories, bonds of blood, such things. If Krishna were to just tell him, 'Arjuna, fighting Duryodhana and killing him is important to uphold *Dharma*,' Arjuna would not fight. Arjuna is not Krishna; Arjuna is not perfect. Family matters are very significant to Arjuna. He cannot forget the insult meted out to Draupadi; he cannot forget that once he used to play in the lap of Bhishma. These kinds of things, they are what are important and material to Arjuna. How do you just tell Arjuna, 'Arjuna, get up and fight! We are crusading for *Dharma*, no less!'? Arjuna would not budge.

So, knowing very well what kind of a person Arjuna is, Krishna is telling Arjuna the things that matter to him. What matters to him? One of the things that matter to him is fame, so Krishna tells him, 'You run away from the battle, and you will be earning a lot of infamy!' Now, *that* matters to Arjuna. 'That is true, I cannot run away—I will be dishonoured! Fine . . .'

Tell Arjuna, 'If you run away, it will be the defeat of *Dharma*!' and such argument will fall flat. Tell Arjuna, 'If you run away, it will be your personal dishonour!' and this argument will work because Arjuna is Arjuna, a normal mortal being.

That, however, does not mean that fame is in reality something very important. That does not mean that fame has some kind of an absolute significance in spirituality. In fact, look at the danger. Krishna is using Arjuna's predisposition towards fame to make him fight a war. It's just that the person right now advising Arjuna is Krishna; he will use Arjuna's weakness to guide him towards the right thing. But what if it were not Krishna but somebody else, and that somebody else knew very well that Arjuna has a very high consideration for fame? Then he could say, 'Arjuna, you lose your fame if you fight against your brothers and uncles and teachers and grandfathers. You will lose your fame!' And Arjuna, fame conscious as he is, would be fooled into quitting the battle because of the fame issue.

It's just that right now Arjuna is in the hands of Krishna—luckily in the hands of Krishna—so Krishna, even though he is using Arjuna's weakness, is using it for the right cause. But what if by way of chance Arjuna were to fall in the hands of somebody like Shakuni? Then Shakuni would capitalize all of Arjuna's weakness to turn Arjuna against *Dharma*.

So, you must understand that it is not at all right to harbour any such weaknesses. And having a soft spot for fame, being very, very desirous for name and honour, is a big weakness. Arjuna is just somehow luckily getting away with it. Not everybody is going to be so lucky. Your hunger for fame will be used by the forces of mischief to turn you to all the wrong directions, so do not wait for that to happen. You will not always be so lucky or so very discreet that your companion would be a Krishna. More often than not, your companions will be of the mischievous and unworthy kind, and they will use all your frailties, all your weaknesses against you and against *Dharma*. Do not let that happen. Get rid of your weaknesses before they are exploited by cunning people.

Then the first part of the question, the connection of infamy with one's actions. The questioner is asking, 'Does a righteous action need to be influenced by how the world perceives it?'

You see, it doesn't need to be, but that's the way we are. We are so thoroughly influenced by the world. While we are deciding about anything, whether to do it or not, the factor of honour, of fame, of perception, of social regard always somehow seeps into the equation. And many a time the question of fame and honour very strongly disbalances the equation. You might be making the right decision, but the factor of infamy starts weighing upon your mind, and then you flip, the decision changes.

The one who gives the opinion of others a lot of weightage will obviously not be able to give the highest weightage to the Truth. Therefore, if you are really someone who aspires to live truthfully, if you are someone who doesn't want to live blindly, semiconscious, then you have to be someone who has a healthy disregard towards the opinions of others. That doesn't mean that you must not hear others out or consult others; rather that means that even if you are listening to others, your objective is not to gain something in the eyes of that person; your objective is to gain the Truth.

You could be listening to your neighbour for two reasons. One, if you listen to your neighbour, your neighbour will feel happy; if you listen to your neighbour, your neighbour will start thinking good things about you. That could be one reason. The other reason is: you are listening to uncover the Truth. And to uncover the Truth, you are prepared to listen to anybody—but *only* to uncover the Truth. Otherwise, people have no value. It is a very strong condition.

Otherwise, what is the value of a body? Nothing. If there is someone who really brings Truth to your life, he is someone to be listened to; heed his advice. And if there are people who are very full of their opinions and are very desirous of advising you but their advice brings no Truth to your life, there is no need to waste your time listening to them.

So, do interact with others, do take feedback from others, do hear people out, do engage in meaningful conversations. But the objective has to be very clear: the objective must always be Truth; not the aggrandization of your ego, not the gratification of the other's ego. No petty objective should be there.

Let people have value in your life only in context of the Truth they bring to your life.

29

Is It Possible to Work Without Expecting Results?

Gita Samagam, BodhSthal, 2020

Fulfillment of expectations does not give you fulfillment. Expectations might get fulfilled; you do not get fulfilled.

~

कर्मण्येवाधिकारस्ते मा फलेषु कदाचन ।
मा कर्मफलहेतुर्भूर्मा ते सङ्गोऽस्त्वकर्मणि ॥

Your right is for action alone, never for the results. Do not become the agent of the results of action. May you not have any inclination for inaction.
—Shrimad Bhagavad Gita, Chapter 2, Verse 47

~

Questioner (Q): I was reflecting on my life in the context of this verse, which says that work should be done without attachment to the fruit.

However, I go to the office and work for money; I learn music for pleasure; I read the scriptures for freedom; I exercise for health; I practise *yogāsanas, prāṇayama, dhyāna* for peace and health; I interact with people and family for pleasure, peace, and security. There's nothing that I do which is not for some gain, and if I am convinced that I will not get what I am expecting out of my action, most probably I will not do it.

How can this be changed in the light of Shri Krishna's wisdom?

Acharya Prashant (AP): All this will not suddenly change in the light of Shri Krishna's wisdom. For the change to happen, first of all, you must have an Arjuna-like self-doubt, and faith in somebody beyond yourself like Krishna.

You say you go to the office and work for money. Does money give you what you want? Unless you come up with at least a doubt regarding the utility of money to your utmost self, no wisdom is going to be of any help to you. If you are someone who says, 'I go to the office and work, I get money in return, and that completes the loop, I am okay. I worked, I got remunerated—I am happy!', then no wisdom will work for you because you are requiring, needing no wisdom. You are entering into a deal and the deal appears profitable to you. Where is the question of moving on to something else?

Similarly, you say you interact with people and family for pleasure, peace, and security. Do you really get peace? Do you *really* get peace? Does the pleasure suffice? Are you *really* secure with respect to the people you are mentioning here?

You say you read scriptures for freedom. The freedom that you imagine that you will get from scriptures, is it really freedom? Or is it a part of your little self? The freedom that your little self imagines, envisages, will it suffice to free the little self of itself?

But here you talk as if the cause-and-effect cycle is serving you beautifully. You say, 'I do something, I get the results, and it is also nice.' If it is also nice, then why do you need the

Gita? The Gita is not for those who are smug and settled in the niceness of their patterns. The law of karma, the teaching of *niṣkāma-karma*, begins at the point of dissatisfaction.

For that matter, all spirituality is only for the dissatisfied ones. The ones who are cool and cozy and contended, I always tell them to carry on. Cool, cozy, contended? Continue, continue! It is an animal-like state in which you do not have any inner turbulence, any deep discontentment, and, therefore, you have no vision, no desire for a greater self.

That's a characteristic of an animal, is it not? Do animals ever experience any kind of existential angst? Do they? Ever heard a buffalo contemplating the meaning of life? Would be quite a pretty picture, by the way. 'B' for buffalo, and the buffalo is saying, 'To "B" or not to "B"? Am I really a buffalo? Because to "B" is to be a buffalo . . .' Or some monkey questioning whether the tree really exists. That doesn't happen; they are all all right.

There is no need to forcefully disturb someone who is feeling all right. It is too messy an affair, and often worthless. Is it worth it to intrude into somebody's peace—howsoever superficial or artificial it is—and shake him up when he doesn't want to be shaken up? The effort may not be worth it; there might be better candidates to teach, to bring up, to support.

Either the questioner has mentioned half the story, in which case he is either not fully honest or does not trust me fully, or if this is the complete story as per the questioner, then the story is nice. Let the story continue!

'I go to the office and work for money.' Happy-shappy! What kind of juvenile story is this? Is this what happens in your office? You go to the office, you work, and get money. Is that the complete story, the total picture? Anybody who has ever entered the workplace even for one day knows that this is not even a fraction of the total psychological happening. There is much more that happens at the workplace. Why don't you tell us about that?

Yes, it is true that you went to the office expecting money. But what did you get? Yes, it is true that you expected money, expecting that money will give you That (referring to fulfillment). Did money give you That? Maybe your expectation that work will give you money was fulfilled. But why are you hiding from me that there was another expectation? The expectation was that money will give you That. Did that expectation materialize? Did that happen?

Further, you are presenting it as if it is some kind of a one-to-one linear mapping between work and money. When you say you go to the office and work and you get money, is it only money that you get from the office? First thing. Secondly, do you get money necessarily for work? Answer both the questions.

First, when you go to the office and work, there is much more than money that you get. Maybe you are not conscious of all that you are obtaining when you are at your workplace, but there is much, much more: all kinds of nonsense, blemishes, rubbish, stress, comparisons, and anxiety.

Equally, when you get paid, is it only because you worked? There are so many who get paid not because they work but because they know a few other skills. Is it really a one-to-one kind of mapping? It is not. It is a complex situation that you are presenting in a deceptively simplistic way.

Shri Krishna is for those who come to see that their expectations are, firstly, not being fulfilled, and more scarily, even when their expectations are being fulfilled, it is not giving them fulfillment. It is a great discovery to come to: Fulfillment of expectations does not give you fulfillment. Expectations might get fulfilled; you do not get fulfilled.

Expectation is *kamana*, desire, and when you see that even the complete fulfillment of expectation gives you neither fulfillment nor completeness, then you say that *kamana* or expectation is junk, I do not want to chase it any further. Only then.

Therefore, this verse is only for those who have, first of all, seen the futility of their self-centric endeavours, those who have seen that we hardly ever get to fulfil our expectations, and more importantly, even when the expectations get fulfilled, we do not get fulfilled. Then Shri Krishna comes into the picture. How does he come into the picture?

The basic trouble is that the point from where the expectations are arising—that which you call as the mind or the self or the ego—is in itself a defective machine to trust so much. We are expecting fulfillment or perfection from the output of a machine that is in itself highly imperfect and incomplete. In fact, the very name of that machine is incompletion.

Now, from the product or the output of such a machine, we expect completion. It is not going to happen. We set a goal, we achieve that goal, then we want fulfillment from the achievement. First of all, where did the goal come from? Who told you that a particular goal is suitable for you? Who told you who you are? Who is the one deciding on the self-identity and setting the goal?

This deciding authority is in itself quite foolish, and that is a discovery one has to make for himself. In that discovery, really no teacher, no agency can assist you; you have to come to life's disappointments on your own. And better for you that you come to them as soon as possible, as early in your life as possible. Once you come to them, then it is possible for you to have a shift of the centre itself. Then you say that the one who is setting the goal is setting the goal for itself, but the one setting the goal does not know how to set the goal; therefore, whatsoever goal it will set will not be of any use for itself; therefore, there is at least one thing I can do now: I will not set the goal for the sake of the goal-setter.

Otherwise, normally, whatsoever goal we set, we set it for our own sake, hoping that the attainment of the goal will do us some good. That is the only purpose behind all goals, right? 'If I reach that goal, then I will have some profit, some betterment, some welfare coming my way.'

The one who enters the first steps of wisdom says, 'The way to get rid of this defective thing inside me is to not honour the goals that it sets for itself. The way to get rid of this thing inside me, this thing that troubles me so much, vexes me endlessly, is to not trust the desires that it generates for me. How do I do that? By not desiring too much for myself.'

So, 'I go to the office and work for money.' For sure, if you will work in the office, you will get a pay cheque. Now, what is the pay cheque being used for? The story doesn't end at the receipt of the pay cheque, or does it? You deposited it, now it is going to be spent and consumed.

The one who realizes Niṣkāma-karma Yoga says, 'I will not spend the money on my own desires. Fine, the cheque has come my way, but let the money be spent on something beyond me to the extent possible, as much as possible—in fact, a little more than as much as possible.'

The little self wanted the money just for its own gratification, and it thought that gratification equals fulfillment: 'Money will come. I will buy a new sofa-set this month! And what will the sofa-set give me?' Oh well, the ego does not put it in so many words, but that's what it implicitly expects or assumes. 'The sofa-set will deliver me emancipation; the sofa-set will mean some kind of *nirvāṇa*; the sofa-set will give me so much happiness. The sofa-set, the furniture is worth slogging the month for. Ultimately, what did I do? I got the pay cheque. Then there are fixed monthly expenses depending on the cost structure I have built for myself, and then there is a particular amount that I put into saving, and after that, all the remainder went into the sofa-set.'

What was the expectation? 'I am putting all my available cash this month into the sofa-set!' Surely, it is foolish when I put it so bluntly. Sounds so very unacceptable, doesn't it? You say, 'No, no, no! We are not such idiots that we will expect liberation from the purchase of a sofa-set!' Consciously, maybe you do not have that expectation. But subconsciously, the sofa-set does mean a lot to you, does it not?

Fine, stretch the sofa-set example a little: let the sofa-set turn into an entire house. For decades you carry the plough just to get a house, don't you? I mean, what else is *sādhanā*? Every day you went to the office, you worked so that you could get some money, and all the remainder after your usual monthly expenses went into the purchase of the house. Surely, you must be having great expectations from the house, right?

That is how the little self operates. It does not just want money; it thinks that the money it earns can deliver something beyond money to it. Something that is just beyond the scope of all work, all action, all material, the little self expects to be delivered through money.

To listen to Krishna is to know that money, when spent in the service of the ego, just inflates the ego and deepens its pre-existing illness. So, money has to be spent in a way that dissolves the ego. That is the rightful use of money.

So, you work, you get money. Some money is obviously needed for your basic physical sustenance, for your basic securities. And then, the surplus has to be spent for a higher cause, not for your own little gratification, not for the kind of titillation that most people are found indulging in.

Now, the catch there is that when you spend money on something tangible—and ego knows only tangibles because ego itself is a material thing. Ego knows only tangibles, and to work for your liberation is to spend money in an intangible way, towards an intangible objective. The ego resists; it says it is foolishness: 'Where is the money going? It is my hard-earned money! What am I really getting by spending it?'

The ego does not realize that even as it is resisting the intangible, it is the intangible that it deeply craves for, that it is actually in love with. Is there any tangible thing that can really satisfy the ego? Is that your experience?

So, the ego, knowing very well that no tangible thing really suffices, still resists when money goes in the direction of the intangible. That resistance has to be either overcome or overlooked.

Similarly, there are other things that come your way by the dent of your basic existence, your day-to-day activities. For example, you say you learn music for pleasure. Can you learn music for a higher purpose? Just as the money you obtain must not go towards the worship of the ego, similarly the knowledge and skills that you attain in music must not be directed towards the gratification of the ego. And it is quite possible, rather easy to do that, is it not?

Look at most people who, for example, learn to play the guitar. What is their objective? And it is mostly the youngsters who go after it. What do they do the moment they have attained even a basic proficiency? You just carry the guitar, get yourself photographed, learn a few basic tunes, impress girls or impress boys, whatever. It all looks so romantic, doesn't it? A guitar by a bonfire, a bonfire by a river on a chilly night, and some idiot is humming *purani jeans aur guitar* (popular Bollywood song, translates to 'old trousers and a guitar'). That is the use we put music to, don't we? And the same music can be an instrument of something far bigger, far more significant.

See how saints used music. So many of them sang, didn't they? Were they using music to fatten their own ego? Were they? Now, that is one way of using music, and the other way is: 'See, now I am the centre of the party: everybody is looking at me!'

In fact, the guitar teachers do not even care about the classical knowledge of the chords, etc., because that is not what most people anyway want. Most people come and say, 'You tell us how to play this particular song, a particular song that is hot these days.' So, there is a list of ten or twenty songs, and whatever the musical code from them is there, that is provided, and the fellow learns to do the strings. Done.

What are you using your music for? That's the question. Are you dedicating it to the service of your little, petty, thirsty ego, or can you be a little more conscious, bigger, wider?

Then, 'I interact with people and family for pleasure, peace, and security.' You forgot to add that you get neither of the three.

Everybody interacts. Anybody here who has never interacted with family members or neighbours or within a friend circle? How many of you got these things? You probably did get pleasure, but a lower kind of pleasure. Did you get some higher bliss—classically called ānanda—by chitchatting, gossiping? What kind of security do you get?

To the extent I know, any little bit of security that is there in your mind disappears the moment you start gossiping with relatives, etc. The moment you are told that Vermaji's Rahul is returning from Canada and very soon he would be married to some girl coming from a fat moneybag father, you start wondering about your own girl and boy. Where is peace, where is security?

The same interactions can have a different purpose, a different ambience altogether. It is a tricky affair. To talk sense with family members is the most difficult thing to do. You might be a university professor, you might have a PhD in logic, but try talking logic to your husband or wife. Very difficult. And even if you can talk logic with your husband, how will you ever talk logic with your husband's mother? Next to impossible but do give it a try.

If it can't be a great purpose, let it at least be greater than what it currently is. Even if you have to interact with someone for just two minutes, can the interaction be higher than what it usually is? See whether it is possible.

The central thing is: Whatever we do, we do for a purpose. Let the purpose be a great purpose.

30

Bonded Work Is Compensation, Free Work Is Compassion

Gita Samagam, BodhSthal, 2020

You cannot run away. Shunning action is not possible. You have to fight. The world is the battlefield. To be born is to be born as a warrior, to be born is to be born with weapons and armour.

~

यस्त्वात्मरतिरेव स्यादात्मतृप्तश्च मानवः ।
आत्मन्येव च सन्तुष्टस्तस्य कार्यं न विद्यते ॥

न बुद्धिभेदं जनयेदज्ञानां कर्मसङ्गिनाम् ।
जोषयेत्सर्वकर्माणि विद्वान्युक्तः समाचरन् ॥

The man who rejoices only in the Self and is satisfied with the Self, and is contented only in the Self—for him there is no duty to perform.

The wise man established in the Self should not unsettle the mind of the ignorant one attached to action, but should get them to perform all their duties while dually performing his own duties.

—Shrimad Bhagavad Gita,
Chapter 3, Verse 17 and 26

~

Questioner (Q): In verse 17, Shri Krishna says that there is no duty to perform for the one who rejoices only in the Self.

However, when we look at the greats like Mahavira, Buddha, or Kabir Sahib, we see that they took huge steps to dispel the darkness of man's mind, as if they were performing an undeclared duty. What makes a Buddha or a Mahavira do what they do?

Also, in verse 26, Shri Krishna again refers to the wise one, and says that he should get others to perform all their duties while dually performing his own. Is there any contradiction here?

Acharya Prashant (AP): You see, Shri Krishna is presenting the entirety, the totality of the matter of action here. On one hand, he says that in the highest state of liberation there is no duty, no *kartavya* left at all. That is point one that you have to understand. At the same time, he says, 'Look at Me, Pārtha (Arjuna)! Who can bind Me in duty? I have no duty at all, and yet I keep doing everything.' He presents his own example. You have to look at everything together to get the complete picture.

On one hand, he indeed says that the liberated one has really no obligation upon him to do anything; the liberated one has no obligation to do anything because he is now liberated. And then he says, 'Look at Me, Pārtha! I keep on doing stuff day in and day out!' and he devotes a couple of verses elaborating how much he does.

He says, 'If I do not do things, this entire world will collapse, so I do more than anybody else. People work in their limited ways. Look at Me, Arjuna! I work in an unlimited way. My labour knows no limits. Nobody works harder than I do!' Arjuna is puzzled. 'But sir, didn't You just say that the liberated one has no duties left to perform? Why do You act then?' Shri Krishna just smiles. 'If you could understand that much, why would you need the Gita?'

So, the common person has duties because he is not liberated, and the liberated one puts duties upon himself *because* he is liberated. That's the way it is. The one in shackles has to bear *kartavya* or duties as punishment; you will have to live within your duties because you are not liberated. This is your punishment. And the liberated one loads himself with duties not because he is full of passion towards the world but because he has compassion.

Shri Krishna tells Arjuna: the *jñāni*, the realized one, should work or rather works in an outwardly way, in a worldly way, just as the ignorant one does. These are very beautiful verses. All the chapters of the Gita are wonderful, but chapter three probably stands the tallest.

He says, 'The ignorant ones keep working, Arjuna. In a similar way, the realized one should also keep working,' and he quotes himself as the foremost example of the worker. He says, 'Look at Me! Here are all the ignorant ones assembled in the field of Kurukshetra to fight. They are working, to fight is their work. And here am I as well. What am I doing in the middle of this idiotic crowd? All fools ready to cut each other to pieces, totally stupid people they are—right on both sides! Do they know why they are fighting? Half of them would be dead before the end of the day! But look at them: how they flex their muscles, how they brandish their weapons, somebody is blowing the conch, somebody is puffing his chest, somebody is threatening the other one. And before the sun sets, half of them will be gone—and gone for nothing! Idiots. And in the middle of this crowd, who is standing as a mere charioteer? Not even a warrior—a charioteer! Me! Me! Doesn't it occur to you, Arjuna, what I am doing here? After all, I am a realized being, am I not?' No, Arjuna is not quite sure about it till Krishna displays to him what is commonly known as the *virāṭ rūpa* (universal form). Krishna is asking, 'What am I doing here? They are fighting because they are ignorant. I am fighting because I am not ignorant.'

That is the way the realized one has to live. Outwardly, it will appear as if he is doing all the things that all the ignorant ones are doing. He cannot shun action; he cannot run away. That is the message: you cannot run away. They are fighting, you too fight. They are fighting from their darkness; you fight from your light. You cannot run away. Shunning action is not possible. You have to fight. The world is the battlefield. To be born is to be born as a warrior, to be born is to be born with weapons and armour. What to do?

Now you know why a Buddha, a Mahavira, a Kabir works so hard all his life. Don't you wonder? What does he have left to achieve? *(Pointing at various people in the audience)* I mean, he's working because he wants a new car, he's working because he wants a new wife, he's working because he wants a new job. What is it that impels the sage to work so hard? That's the secret. That's what made Krishna smile.

'Arjuna, you will never really know why I work because I work without a why. You work for a reason; I work for no reason. And if you have to have a reason, the reason is compassion. You know, you are a man of words. You need some word to satisfy your shallow inquiry, so I give you a word: the word is "compassion".'

If you go to Kabir Sahib, he will say the word is *sahajatā* (naturalness). The realized one just works. He doesn't work for a cause, really. Though apparently, he might declare a cause. He will say, 'You know, I am working for such and such reasons, for such a cause, for such a mission,' such things. But really, he's just working—*just* working. He cannot help it. It has to happen. You cannot go to him and question, 'But why are you doing it?'

Somebody went to J. Krishnamurti, who was saying one doesn't need a teacher or a guru and one is sufficient unto himself and such things. And there was this person, he questioned Krishnamurti. He said, 'But aren't you teaching as well? You, too, are a de facto guru, and all the time you are railing against gurus!' Krishnamurti was almost shocked, it is said. You know how he replied? He said, almost as if caught or accused or convicted, 'But I don't do it intentionally!'

That's how the realized one acts. He doesn't do it intentionally. He just acts. He *just* acts.

Somewhere, if I remember correctly, Krishnamurti also said, 'When the flower blooms, the fragrance spreads.' The flower doesn't really intend to make your day; it just happens. The flower can't help it. The flower didn't really plan to entertain your nostrils or your mind; it just happens. That's the state of the realized one. He can't help it; he is helpless.

'Oh! Bad! But we thought he is quite empowered; we thought that if you are realized, then you are all in control of yourself!' Oh no, not at all. Rather, what you call as realization is about losing all self-control: you just flow—flow not in the way the common man flows.

The common man flows in the dirty stream of his passions and desires and tendencies. The flow of the realized one is an altogether different thing; it is a different stream. A few years back, I had differentiated between the two streams, calling one stream as accidental and the other as essential.

But, you know, some smart fellow can actually go to Kurukshetra and accost Krishna: 'Sir, what are you doing here? After all, you are Krishna! Your place is in the jungle! And if not in the jungle, you should be found at some other quiet, secluded place meditating or perfecting your yoga. After all, you are the supreme yogi, aren't you? How does it behoove a yogi to have the harness in his hand?'

(Reading the question again) 'Is there a contradiction here? What makes a Buddha or a Mahavira do what they do?'

No, no contradiction here. And do not ask for a reason. If you are really honest, then you should know that there does not exist a reason. As we said, if you are interested in satisfying your flimsy curiosity, then you could say the reason is the upliftment of the world. As they say in common usage, the sage takes birth to redeem the world, but that is the language of the world. In the sage's own language, such an expression does not exist. He will not say that he has come to serve the world or redeem the world or do some favour to the world. He just does what he does. This 'justness' is the pinnacle of all spiritual advancement, *sahajatā*.

Even Krishna does not really disclose to Arjuna why he runs the entire world or maintains the *prakritik* (natural) order. He does not disclose. He just says, 'I do that, I do that,' and Arjuna is probably not insouciant enough to insist on an answer, so he lets it be at that.

Q: Just now, you said that the liberated one doesn't do anything intentionally, he just does it, whereas the non-liberated one acts with a cause. Is there a reason behind it?

AP: There can be two reasons there.

You see, if you are someone who is in bondage, then your actions could be in two directions. The direction of the irreligious action is towards the thickening or deepening of your bondages. Then there is the religious action: that is called *kartavya*. What is *kartavya* or *Dharma*? That which leads to freedom from your bondages.

So, these two courses of action are possible to the one who is not yet liberated. He can act this way, or he can act that way.

Then there is the liberated one. The liberated one really does not need to act for himself because he has no bondages left. He does not need to liberate himself further. He is already liberated, yet he keeps on working—and that's what the wonder is.

If the one in shackles acts, then it can be explained: he is acting for the sake of his freedom, liberation. He is in shackles. You can see the chains, the fetters. So, he is working, and it is obvious why he is working. He is a sincere fellow; he is a sensible fellow. He wants freedom. This is the religious man.

Who is the irreligious man? He who is wearing chains and working in a way that will load him with more bondages. This is the irreligious fellow.

Now, you come to the liberated one. The liberated one needs no religion at all; he has gone beyond religion. In his case, religion has already served its purpose. He needs no religion. Does Krishna follow a religion? No. Krishna is religion itself. He does not follow any religion.

There is no *Dharma*, no *kartavya* for Krishna, and yet he is found working so very diligently, so very uninterruptedly. Why? That's what you need to find out. In trying to find that out, the finder will get lost. That's the great thing about such an endeavour to find. No finding will really happen, but the one who set out to find will get exhausted.

Q: If the liberated one stops doing work because it is not his compulsion to act, will it then leave no difference between the liberated and the non-liberated?

AP: How will he stop doing? Who will force him to stop doing? He does what he does. He is alone to himself. Who can stop him from doing what he must? It is his free will—and *only* he really has free will. You cannot stop him. You can at most physically kill him—go ahead and do that! But still, you cannot really stop him. He will express himself in some other way. The spirit will remain. One instance of the spirit, one particular body can be killed, but the spirit really cannot be stopped.

Liberation is not something that happens to a man. It is more abstract; there is nothing personal. Therefore, I keep saying that the way we usually talk about enlightenment is all bogus. Enlightenment is a myth.

The liberated one loads himself with duties not because he is full of passion towards the world but because he has compassion.

31

The Fine Line between
Sāttvika and *Tāmasika* Action

Gita Samagam, BodhSthal, 2020

You are your desire; you are the quality of your desire.
Just see what you are getting. Just see which relationships
are strengthening. Just see who you are drifting away
from. Just see where you are found. Just see where you are
not found. Just see what ultimately is the result of all this.

~

नियतं सङ्गरहितमरागद्वेषतः कृतम् ।
अफलप्रेप्सुना कर्म यत्तत्सात्त्विकमुच्यते ॥

यत्तु कामेप्सुना कर्म साहङ्कारेण वा पुनः ।
क्रियते बहुलायासं तद्राजसमुदाहृतम् ॥

अनुबन्धं क्षयं हिंसामनपेक्ष्य च पौरुषम् ।
मोहादारभ्यते कर्म यत्तत्तामसमुच्यते ॥

An ordained action done without love or hatred by one
not desirous of the fruit and free from attachment is
declared to be sāttvika.

But that action which is performed desiring results, or
with self-conceit and with much effort, is declared to
be rājasika.

187

That action is declared to be tāmasika which is undertaken through delusion, without heed to the consequence, loss (of power and wealth), injury (to others), and to (one's own) ability.

—Shrimad Bhagavad Gita,
Chapter 18, Verses 23 to 25

Questioner (Q): Shri Krishna says *sāttvika* action is done without desire for the fruit, and then he says *tāmasika* action is done through delusion, without paying heed to consequences.

It seems Shri Krishna has drawn a very fine line here. Please help me understand the right action in light of the above verses.

Acharya Prashant (AP): So, on the one hand, Shri Krishna is saying here that in *sāttvika* action you do not care for the results. On the other hand, the *tāmasika* person, too, has been defined as the one who does not care for the result; he continues in his self-destructive ways without caring for the results at all.

So, the questioner is asking, what is this fine line that Shri Krishna seems to have drawn here? Good question.

You see, there are two reasons, two possibilities, two scenarios where you don't care for the results. One is because you know that you are absolutely right, so now you have no option left. Therefore, there is no point caring for the results. This is the only thing that you can rightly do, so what is the point in talking or bothering so much about the results? That is one possibility. That is the *sāttvika* possibility. You are deeply contented just doing what you are doing. It is all right now.

Then there is the *tāmasika* person. The *tāmasika* person is compelled to not care for the results for reasons that are totally opposite to the *sāttvika* case. The *tāmasika* person gets deeply bitter and harmful results for being what he is and doing what he does because that is the nature of his being. Everything that he does actually brings him hurtful consequences. Now it is extremely important for him to not care for those consequences if he is to continue remaining the deluded one that he currently is. Otherwise, the very force of the results would show him a mirror; the very tribulations of life would compel him to change. But he doesn't want to change. Therefore, what is his tagline? 'I don't care for the results.'

This is not his joy. This is his compulsion. He will have to deliberately and stubbornly ignore the results because the results are shrieking to him, 'You are living a very bad life!' The moment he pays attention to the results he will have to change, but his deep and unyielding ego refuses to change even while suffering deeply. That is *tāmasikta*.

What is the definition of the *tāmasikta*? You are in the wrong place and you don't even want to leave that place. You are living badly and you are saying, 'This is what is called the right life.'

That is why the *rājasika* mind is better than the *tāmasika* mind. The *rājasika* mind says, 'I am not all right; I need to do something to become better. I feel inferior, I feel incomplete; I need to rise, I need to achieve.' That is the *rājasika* mind. The *rājasika* mind at least admits that it is not all right, that it needs to change and improve, though it tries to improve in an unwise and foolish way. But at least that admission is there. 'I am not all right.'

The *tāmasika* mind is a tough nut to crack. 'I am all right.' 'But you're not all right.' 'But I am all right!' 'But you are unhappy!' 'Oh, I am joyful.' 'But last night you were wailing and sobbing!' 'In that is my pleasure!' That kind of an argument. 'I made a video. You are frothing from the mouth and flowing in the eye. Your face was just froth and tears, and you are cursing your life. Here, I shot it!' And what does the fellow say? 'In that is my pleasure. I love to wail; I love to yell. I love to shriek; I love to cry. Tears give me a high!'

And now, how do you talk to this fellow? He says, 'I am all right. I am all right as I am.' In his own eyes he is some goddamn philosopher—especially after he is a bit high. It is very, very important for him—it is a matter of survival—to not care about the results, to not even inquire into the results. The day he starts inquiring into the results, he will be forced to change.

Therefore, I deeply oppose this neo-pop spiritual culture of living in the present. I do not want people to not care about the results because not caring for results is all right only if you are a *sāttvika* mind or if you have transcended the ego. Then it is all right to not care for results. But if you are a *rājasika* person or a *tāmasika* person—as 99.9 per cent of people are—then you need to be very, very conscious of the future and the results of your actions.

The *tāmasika* mind desperately wants to avoid looking at the consequences of his actions. That is the reason why the saints, if you visit their literature, constantly reminded us to think of the results of our actions and of death. They kept saying, 'Think of death.' Now, all that is in the future, but today's pop spirituality is about ignoring the future totally. 'Don't think of the future, live in the present!' Then why were the saints continuously telling us to think of death? Death is always in the future, right now you aren't dead.

It is because the saints knew better; they knew who they were talking to. They knew they were talking to *rājasika* and *tāmasika* minds, and they need to be cautioned of the future. That's the *tāmasika* mind's ultimate fantasy: to do what he wants to do and then not bear the consequences. Is that not a great fantasy? 'I will do what I want to do; I will consume what I want to consume, and I won't even have to foot the bill!'

The saints are saying the bill will need to be paid—with due interest. Mind the bill!

It is a very unfortunate trend these days, living in the now, living in the present. No wonder it is coming from the centre of consumerism and is only serving to promote it. 'Consume right now, don't worry about the consequences!' No wonder the country this cult is coming from is the most debt-ridden country in the world. No wonder the society this cult is coming from carries the highest per capita debt on its head. Do you know about the average credit card dues of the common American? They are the highest in the world. 'Spend on your credit card. Live in the present. Don't worry about the future.'

In fact, the 2008 crisis was, in many ways, a crisis of credit. Loans had been given to people who were in no condition to pay them back. And what did those people do with those loans? They lived in the present. They enjoyed that money to not think about the future and to be joyful in the present. And when the banks wanted their money back, there was no money to be had back. The banks didn't know what to do, and then they started rolling one after the other, declaring bankruptcy. On paper, they all had a lot of assets: 'So much has been lent to this person, and that person owes so much to me.' All that was on paper. In reality, nothing—because those debts had all been happily consumed. So, when the bank said, 'Please return my money . . .' *(Shrugs)* That is 'now', 'in the present'!

Be very conscious of your action and its results.

You know, sometimes people ask me, 'How do we know where our actions are coming from? You keep on talking about the importance of acting from the right centre. But how exactly do we determine the centre our action is coming from?'

And I say, the centre your actions are coming from is probably a bit hidden. It is an inner thing, and you don't have the eyes to look inwards. But you can at least pay attention to the results of your action. And when you do that, here is a formula for you: the result of your action is the exact point your action is coming from; the source of your action is exactly the same as the consequence of your action.

So, watch the consequences of your actions, and you will realize what the source of the action is. If you have done something, just figure out what the net result of that entire activity or episode was, and then you should know that the entire episode happened just for the sake of that particular result. That was your hidden intention.

For example, you do something, and in some convoluted way, finally it leads you to break away from a friend. That is the net output of that episode. Now, if you have to ask, 'Where did my actions come from?' then you should know that your action actually came from your subconscious desire to get rid of that friend. That is all that you wanted.

The beginning is the end. The result is the source. If you cannot know the source, know the result.

We are very complicated and deceitful beings. You will never know why you are acting in a particular way because you do not want to admit that to yourself. But one good way of realizing why you act as you act is to just see the final result of what you are doing. Obviously, you can turn back and say there is nothing called a final result. All right, then look at the intermediate result. It is for the sake of that intermediate result that you are doing what you are doing.

Nothing happens coincidentally in the realm of the ego, for the ego is the doer. The ego doesn't let things happen; it does them. It doesn't let things happen, does it?

So, when you are doing something, rest assured that the output is something that the ego wanted. Even if the output appears shocking, even if you want to claim that it is quite an unintended output or outcome, that unintended outcome is not really unintended. You wanted it. You caused it. But you caused it in a very hidden way, in a very abstruse way because you didn't want to admit to yourself that you are directly or intentionally doing it.

And that is one solid reason why you must mind the consequences: because the consequence will tell you about your centre. If you look even at the gross actions and their results carefully, you will come to know of the subtle forces operating within.

So, something has been happening with you over the last one month, let's say, and you narrate the entire story to someone. If that someone is wise, he will ask, 'All right, what is the net result of all this that has been happening with you?' And you say, 'Well, the net result is . . .' He will say, 'Okay, I will help you out. Compared to one month back, how have things changed for you right now? What has changed?' And you will say, 'All right, now that's easier to answer. These are the three things that have changed over that last one month.'

Then that someone will tell you, 'It is with the intention of changing these three things that you have been acting the way you have over the last one month. It is not that your actions have coincidentally brought about this result; it is because you wanted this result deep within, hence you have been acting the way you have been acting. You are just fulfilling your deep desires.'

So, always ask yourself, 'All this happened ultimately to what result, to what effect, to what end?' Never ignore the consequences. Never.

Keeping a check on the consequences is a great way to self-reflect. Otherwise, how will you know who you are? Unless you know what you desire, how will you know who you are? And how will you know what you desire? By seeing what you get because you are only getting what you are desiring. That's the way of the ego. It proceeds on desire.

So, see what you are getting from life continuously as a result of your actions. That is what you are desiring. And who are you? You are your desire; you are the quality of your desire. Just see what you are getting. Just see which relationships are strengthening. Just see who you are drifting away from. Just see where you are found. Just see where you are not found. Just see what ultimately is the result of all this.

Because stories are complicated, you know. If you get lost in the details of the stories, you will never come to know the truth. So, keep the story aside, just ask for the conclusion. What is the conclusion? What happened as a result of all this that you are trying to tell me? Ask.

'So, this happened and that happened, and then he brought this, then I did this, and then I said that, then he met me there, and then we agreed, and then we disagreed, and then we fought, and then we hugged, and then I sent him this letter, and then he wrote me a mail,' and a thousand things. All right, please conclude. 'Well, you see, then we broke up.'

So, fine. That's it. This is exactly what you wanted, and for the sake of this result you enacted the entire drama. Maybe not intentionally, just subconsciously, but this is the result that you ultimately wanted anyway.

Be particular about the consequences. That is the reason why the wise ones gave us the principle of karma. What did the principle of karma imply? 'Oh, you will have to pay up. You can't go scot-free.' To the layman, the principle of karma is just the principle of consequences. And it is very important that most people are mindful of *karmaphala*. What is *karmaphala*? Consequences. It is only now that the time-tested theory of karma is being rubbished aside in favour of pop theories of 'living in the now', etc.

Living in the now is something very special; only the ones already liberated have the right to live in the now. The others must be very conscious of the future. It is by remaining conscious of the future that you will ultimately get freedom from the future. It is by being extremely conscious that you will gain freedom from consciousness itself. It is by minding your actions and their results that you will ultimately gain freedom from the actor. How else will you gain freedom from the actor? If you do not know the actor, will you be able to be free from the actor?

What is your bondage? Your bondage is ignorance. Your bondage is that you do not know the actor, and that's why there is no freedom from the actor.

And how will you know the actor? The actor is hidden, subtle; the actor doesn't have a face. How do you know the actor? By looking at the actions.

But in one's eyes, his actions are anyway always all right. So, how do you know your actions really? By looking at the results of the actions.

Looking at the results of the actions is one foolproof way to know the actor, and when you know the actor, that gains you freedom from the actor.

Not caring for results is all right only if you are a sāttvika mind or if you have transcended the ego. Then it is all right to not care for results. But if you are a rājasika person or a tāmasika person—as 99.9 per cent of people are—then you need to be very, very conscious of the future and the results of your actions

32

Which Actions Must
One Never Renounce?

Gita Samagam, BodhSthal, 2020

*We want to reach the end of wanting. We want
completion, fulfillment in such a final way that we
are left with nothing to want anymore. That's the
destination.*

~

यज्ञदानतपःकर्म न त्याज्यं कार्यमेव तत् ।
यज्ञो दानं तपश्चैव पावनानि मनीषिणाम् ॥

एतान्यपि तु कर्माणि सङ्गं त्यक्त्वा फलानि च ।
कर्तव्यानीति मे पार्थ निश्चितं मतमुत्तमम् ॥

नियतस्य तु संन्यासः कर्मणो नोपपद्यते ।
मोहात्तस्य परित्यागस्तामसः परिकीर्तितः ॥

दुःखमित्येव यत्कर्म कायक्लेशभयात्त्यजेत् ।
स कृत्वा राजसं त्यागं नैव त्यागफलं लभेत् ॥

कार्यमित्येव यत्कर्म नियतं क्रियतेऽर्जुन ।
सङ्गं त्यक्त्वा फलं चैव स त्यागः सात्त्विको मतः ॥

The work of yagya, gift, and austerity should not be relinquished, but it should indeed be performed; (for) yagya, gift, and austerity are purifying to the wise.

But even these works, O Pārtha, should be performed, leaving attachment and the fruits. Such is My best and certain conviction.

But the renunciation of obligatory action is not proper. Abandonment of the same from delusion is declared to be tāmasika.

He who from fear of bodily trouble relinquishes action, because it is painful, thus performing a rājasika relinquishment, he obtains not the fruit thereof.

When obligatory work is performed, O Arjuna, only because it ought to be done, leaving attachment and fruit, such relinquishment is regarded as sāttvika.

—Shrimad Bhagavad Gita,
Chapter 18, Verses 5 to 9

~

Questioner (Q): It is being said, 'Renunciation of obligatory action is not proper.'

What is meant by obligatory action? Is Shri Krishna talking about my social responsibilities or something else?

Acharya Prashant (AP): No. First of all, the English word 'obligatory' is not quite proper. Shri Krishna says *niyata-karma; niyataṃ karma kuru*. A more befitting word would be 'destined action', not 'obligatory action'. It is not *nirdhārita-karma* (pre-ordained or pre-determined action), it is *niyata-karma*. It is not quite an obligation; it is the only real option. It is your destiny.

You are being advised to do that which your destiny has anyway pre-ordained. And what is that? Social responsibilities? Familial responsibilities? Following the code of your sect, cult, or religion? Following the dictates of your desires and fancies? Is that your destiny? Nobody in his right senses would agree to this.

Destiny is the end. Destiny is the final point for the sake of which we all exist and keep moving. What is it that we finally want? Where is it that we ultimately want to reach? That is destiny, obviously. Destination, the end, the summit, the culmination, the total fulfillment, absolute completion—all these point towards destiny.

So, what is it that we are moving towards? Look at any human being, any conscious being. What is it that they ultimately want? We keep wanting, right? What is the ultimate want? Here is a hint: If the want is really final and ultimate, then it would leave you with no residual or next want.

So, we want to reach the end of wanting. We want completion, fulfillment in such a final way that we are left with nothing to want anymore.

That is the destination. That is what all spiritual process is aimed at: a peace, a contentment so absolute that you are left with no trace of incompleteness, bitterness, hope, future, desire. That is the destiny. That's the destiny because if we don't reach it, we will keep moving. How can you stop if you are still discontent? How can you stop if you are still unfulfilled? You will have to continue your movement just as it has continued since time eternal.

So, if that is the destiny, what is destined action, *niyata-karma*? Destiny is the end of all karma. Then, what is *niyata-karma*? What is destined action? Go into it. You have to act in a way that brings you to your destiny, and destiny is the end of both the actor and action. But destined action is the action that brings you to your destiny, and it can bring you to your destiny only when such action is guided by the destiny alone.

You see, whosoever guides or dictates your action would make you act in a way that suits the guide, that fulfils the aspirations and matches the character of the guide, right? If you are to reach your destiny, then can miscellaneous forces of *Prakriti* (physical nature) be the right guide for your movement? If miscellaneous forces are guiding you, they will direct you towards miscellaneous destinations. Isn't that obvious?

If you are to reach your destiny, then only your destiny can guide you. And if your destiny is Truth, then only Truth can guide you towards Truth, only Truth can illuminate your path towards the Truth. Therefore, your destined action is to get rid of your falsenesses. Act in a way, inspired by the Truth, that you hack down the shackles of your falseness. If your destiny is freedom, then you have to act in a way that negates your bondages. That's what *niyata-karma* is.

Niyata-karma has been widely and grossly misinterpreted and misrepresented. People have said *niyata-karma* is obligatory action, which means you have to do things that society expects of you, or stuff that your culture expects of you, or you have to engage in particular types of behaviour or conduct. This they have named as the obligatory action. It is not, obviously. Your obligation is towards no one except Krishna. Is that not the essence of the Gita?

Even if you are to engage in obligatory action, who is it that you are obliged to? Are you obliged to the priest, the pastor, and to all the runners of the society? What is it that you really owe to them? Nothing! Then how can you be obliged to them?

All that you owe to yourself is your freedom. And you heavily owe that to yourself, don't you? You are indebted to yourself. That's your obligation if we are to talk the language of obligation at all. That is your *only* obligation.

Your only obligation and responsibility, in other words, is to reach your destination. You are not indebted towards anybody else in any serious way. Yes, there are superficial obligations and debts that you must keep settling, that's fine, but all that cannot be taken too seriously. Even if those debts are settled fully, still you would be as deeply mired in misery as you currently are.

Let's say you owe a couple of lakhs (hundred thousand) to someone; let's say there are certain functions to be performed in the family, and you feel responsible for them; let's say you have to provide for somebody's education; let's say you feel that it is very important for you to get somebody married off. Let's say that you are able to take care of all these obligations.

Now, where does that put you? In a very sweet and sacred spot? Are you joyful and content now? The one you wanted to marry off has been married off, the loans that you needed to settle have been settled, the house that you wanted to build has been built. All the obligations that you could think and dream of have indeed now been taken care of. Where does that leave you? Free? Liberated?

So, fine. It is a part of the drama of life that you keep settling some dues. There are no free lunches. If you just have enjoyed a full meal somewhere, it is obligatory upon you to settle the bill. It is all right. Keep doing all those things. But those things can't be taken very seriously because they aren't seriously going to take you to your destination. To go to your destination, your internal compass has to be aligned in a very different way, to a very different field.

Even while performing your so-called daily routine, you have to constantly keep thinking, 'How are my actions directed towards my liberation?' See, you cannot stop certain actions. You will get up, you will take a bath, you will brush your teeth, you will have food, you will need some clothes, you will talk to people, you will need sleep, right? All those things are there. The question is: 'Those things are indispensable, but have I aligned those actions with the greater direction of my liberation?'

Being a human being, you will walk—but which direction are your legs taking you? Being a human being, you will talk—but who is it that you are talking to? Being a human being, you will eat—but how really have you earned your bread? In whose company are you breaking your bread? Those are the questions that you seriously need to answer. Those are the questions that will decide whether you are doing your *niyata-karma*.

Niyata-karma, I repeat, is not about sticking to a particular code of pre-decided conduct. *Niyata-karma* is a very lively and dynamic thing. Every moment you have to be alert and conscious; every moment you have to keep asking yourself, 'This action that I am doing, this decision that I am taking, is it leading me towards liberation, or have I given in to my ego? Where is this coming from, and hence, what is it taking me towards?'

In the middle of all your daily miscellaneous actions, keep asking yourself, 'What is the sum total of all of this? What is the net result? Am I getting lost in the maze of the thousand little things that happen to me daily, or have I retained the insight to see what the net resultant of my entire day is?' And there are a thousand little things that happen to everybody every day. The important thing is to keep the result in mind. 'What is the sum total of all of this?'

Giving undue importance to something micro, something trivial, is quite tempting, and equally tempting is to give little importance to that which deserves tremendous attention. The little things we do every day, I repeat, are unavoidable. What is, however, possible is to align them to the one great thing that we live for.

The man living badly sleeps, wakes up, walks, eats, talks, works, sleeps, and the man living rightly sleeps, wakes up, walks, eats, works, sleeps. They all do the same things, ostensibly. Seen from a distance, apparently both are just living and acting. But go closer and pay attention, and you will find that there is a great difference between talking and talking, eating and eating, earning and earning, walking and walking.

Gautama Buddha was walking the jungles, so were a thousand robbers. An uninitiated eye would not spot the difference. So, one fellow just walked past me; he was Gautama Buddha. Then there is another fellow who walked past me; he was a robber. They are the same because both are just walking. But there is a great difference between walking and walking. When Gautama Buddha is walking, his walk is aligned with his destiny, his walk is being controlled by something beyond the ego. And when the robber is walking, his steps, his walk are being commanded by something very trivial. That's the difference. That alignment is extremely important.

And 'alignment' is a modern and moderate word. In classical spirituality, this alignment of your daily life with your ultimate purpose is called surrender. You do whatever you do, but you surrender it to an ultimate purpose.

So, you do speak, you do shout, you do stand still, and you do run hard; you do all those things. But all those things are now being done at the command of something far bigger than your limited interests, your limited ego. That is called *niyata-karma*.

Never be confused again. *Niyata-karma* is not what the elders have decided for you; *niyata-karma* is not what the traditions have decided for you. *Niyata-karma* is that which takes you to your dissolution; which is your destiny, which is your desire ultimate.

Born a human being, you will have to act. Act rightly. Act for the right purpose. Live for the right end. That alone is the right life.

33

How to Submit One's Actions to Truth?

Course in Realization, BodhSthal, 2017

> *You may give yourself all that you can imagine, and yet you will find that the little personal self is still calling out for more. Give yourself the best of your dreams and fulfil them, give yourself the best that the world can offer, and yet you will find that you haven't come to a full-stop.*

Questioner (Q): One way to live life is to stay alert in each and every moment, and the other way is *Bhaktī Yoga*, which is talked of in texts like the Bhagavad Gita. On this basis, all actions need to be submitted to God, which means remembering God in every action.

Are these two different paths? Do they converge?

Acharya Prashant (AP): The first path that you have mentioned is about staying alert. The second path says, 'Submit all actions to God.' What does that mean?

In general, whenever we act, our actions are for our own sake. Our actions are, therefore, submitted to ourselves. We have a small personal domain, and that is what we take our universe to be. That domain is our universe.

If you look at what your mind has been thinking of, it is not really much: a few friends, a few family members, your job, your future, your little set of memories, your narrow domain

of hopes and expectations and dreams from the future, and
nothing beyond that. There is so much happening in the
universe. It never flashes in our minds. It does not occur to
us, it does not exist for us. We have no space for it.

So, our personal universes are as small as our personal
selves, and all our actions are dedicated to these personal
selves. These personal selves are small and, therefore,
insecure. They are limited and, therefore, defenceless. We
feel threatened and vulnerable all the time, so all our actions
are towards our imagined betterment. 'I am vulnerable, I am
threatened. I need to do something for my upkeep, for my
security.'

If you are not all right, obviously you will act only to
help yourself, to protect yourself, to improve yourself.
And that is what the life of the ordinary so-called normal
human being is: dedicated to his own service. What do you
work for? 'I work for myself. It may appear that I work for
my family, but the fact is I work for these people because
they are related to me. Hence, I am working for myself.
It may appear that I work for an organization, but I work
for that organization because it pays me. The day it stops
paying me, I won't work for it. Hence, I really work only
for myself.'

Our actions are always dedicated to ourselves.

It is rare, almost impossible to find even one action that
has not gone into that infinite sink which is self-service. We
keep on serving ourselves, yet the service is never complete.
The self is so vulnerable, so inexhaustible, and yet so limited
that it keeps absorbing what you offer it and yet is always
hungry, empty, crying for more. You may give yourself all
that you can imagine, and yet you will find that the little

personal self is still calling out for more. Give yourself the best of your dreams and fulfil them, give yourself the best that the world can offer, and yet you will find that you haven't come to a full-stop.

Self-service is an endless road. All our actions are spent down that road.

Now it must be already clear to you what it means to submit all actions to God. It means: do not work for your little personal self. But to not work for your little personal self, you must be in touch with something beyond you. That is an act of courage.

The little self is so terrified—and at the same time so sure of itself—that the moment it comes across something, somebody bigger than itself, beyond itself, something in another dimension, it closes its eyes; it acts as if it has seen nothing. Because if you have seen beyond yourself, you will know that it is not wise to keep acting for your own sake; it is not wise to invest all your efforts, all your life, all your time in the few directions that you are accustomed to.

One needs to have a certain courage, a certain desire, and a certain frustration in order to accept the great, the immense as existent.

There are two mistakes that the personal self makes. One—that most people make—is to pretend that the beyond does not exist. 'Nothing beyond me exists. Life means: my house, my family, my occupation, my little ups and downs, my pains, my pleasures, my desires, my disappointments. That is what life and universe are all about.' This is the first mistake: to act as if nothing beyond you is material or important.

The second mistake is to come across the important, to come across somebody from the beyond, and then try to possess him. This is a more severe mistake, and this is a more tragic mistake. This is a more tragic mistake because it is a case of so near yet so far.

You come across a Jesus, a Krishna, a Buddha, and instead of submitting to him, you try to bring him home. This is the more severe mistake of the two. You try to own him; you try to bring him down to your own dimension; you try to co-opt him; you try to make him a part of your existing system, your existing network, your existing universe.

To submit your actions to God means to come across God and bow down, and to realize that there does exist an aloofness, a beyondness. It is humbling; it is a realization of one's smallness. It hurts—but one does not want to easily admit that. But if you can admit that, you will know what is the right action. If you have really seen something that is not beset with the problems, the frailties that characterize our life, then why not dedicate ourselves to that? That will be the right action.

To find something that is so very immense that neither does it exist in your universe nor can it be adjusted in your personal universe, neither does it exist in your home nor is it adjustable in your home—and by 'home' I mean the place that you feel comfortable in, not only the physical place but the mental place too. Not only is this immense that you have come across beyond your current place, it is also so large that it cannot be contained in your current place. So, any efforts to bring that home are futile.

Hence, the only way out for you, if you want the company of the immeasurable, is that you go to Him. That is what is meant by dedicating your actions to God.

'I am not working for myself anymore. The fruits of my actions will not benefit me, my actions are really for something beyond me. My personal world is not going to benefit from my actions,' because if that happens, you are only strengthening the false; you are only strengthening the person; you are only strengthening your own disease; you are only fattening the enemy.

So, what do you work for? 'I don't know.' Whom do you work for? 'I don't know.' What do you get out of this work? 'I don't bother! If I am someone who is desirous of fruits from my work, then that surely means that I am working from a point of incompleteness. And if I am starting from a point of incompleteness, if that is what I take myself to be, an incomplete one, then the work will have all the characteristics of incompleteness. And such work will obviously not take me to completeness. If I act as the sick one, my actions, too, will have the imprint of sickness, and sick actions will not take me to health.'

The right action is when one is not acting for himself or herself. The right action is when the fruits of the action will dissolve you rather than continue you or strengthen you.

Is it similar to the path of knowledge, to the path of alertness? Of course! As the questioner has mentioned, the path of knowledge entails staying alert, being watchful of oneself. Only then do you come to know that you are acting only for your own petty interests. You may claim that you are acting in love or in charity, but there is always self-interest behind all love, all charity.

No altruism is possible for the ego. The ego is so little and so afraid that it cannot help anybody but itself.

When you are shivering with fear, the interest of others, the welfare of others does not matter to you. A terrified mind will first and foremost be bothered about its own security.

That is what one needs to be alert of. Otherwise, it is easy to be deluded by one's own intentions—self-proclaimed intentions.

You may say, 'I did nothing for myself, and all my life I have been serving you kids!' Have you been serving the kids of the neighbour? Have you been serving the kids from the slum society nearby? But look at the bold assertion: 'I have dedicated my life to my family!' You don't even see the incongruity in the very statement. '*My* family.' You did it because there was ownership. If you are washing or servicing your car, are you doing somebody a favour? If you are charging your mobile phone, is it social service? And there are so many people who feed their kids just as one charges the mobile phone: for use. Why do you charge the mobile phone?

If you are really alert and you look at the world around, is it not so that we feed our relationships because later on, or immediately, we want to be fed by them? Do you maintain relationships that are really of no use to you? Neither physical nor material, not even mental? Do you really maintain any such relationships? Either the relationship offers you something, promises to offer you something, or at least stands for something.

We are very purposeful people. If there is no purpose contained in anything, we drop it. And we delude ourselves. In order to maintain a morally correct self-image, what do we proclaim? 'Oh, we are serving! This is love!' And then there comes a point when you cry out, 'I did so much for you in pure love, and this is what you are offering me in return?' Had it been pure love, would it have come to this statement? Does pure love care for returns? But see how hurt you are when the one you have loved does not fulfil your expectations.

A stranger has very little power to hurt you, but the beloved, the loved one has so much power to hurt you. What does that immediately prove? That you were not just loving; your love was full of expectations. It was hardly love. It was a business deal. 'I will do this for you, and I expect that this is what you will give me.' And when you do not get what you want, you are so hurt. The hurt is the proof of the falseness of our impersonal, unconditional love. Had it really been unconditional, had it really been true and genuine, from where would the hurt have arisen?

Alertness helps. Alertness helps you to see your real motives. In lying to others, and doing so continuously, there comes a point where we start believing in our own propaganda. Four hundred times you have told someone, 'I love you,' and now you yourself feel that you are indeed in love.

You have heard that story, right? There has been a funny Sufi fellow called Mullah Nasruddin. His entire life is a joke book. You must read one of the books dedicated to him. This was his way to tell, to teach, via self-mockery. He would turn himself into a joke and thus teach people. So, he would be dressed in a very bizarre way, and kids and animals are attracted to bizarre things.

One day he was walking in his usual way, and kids got attracted to his funny sight. They all came and started bothering him: somebody started tugging at his shirt, somebody started pulling his sleeve. The ways of kids, as kids are.

When they had pestered him enough, he devised a trick. He said, 'Hey! Listen all of you, little ones! Somebody there in the market is distributing really good sweets. All of you must rush there!'

The kids did not believe. They said, 'No, no, it doesn't happen!' He said, 'No, no, it is happening, you believe me!' And with all kinds of tricks and arguments he somehow convinced them, and the kids went away towards the market.

The Mullah kept watching them for a while as they disappeared, and then started running after them. Somebody was watching the entire show. He stopped Mullah and said, 'Half an hour you invested in somehow getting rid of them. Now you are running after them in the same direction! What are you doing?'

He said, 'Who knows, maybe somebody actually is distributing sweets. After all, if so many of them could believe in this, it might just be true!'

That is the story of our life. We have lied so much that we have come to believe in our own lies. Alertness, therefore, helps. When you look at your life, the bare fact of your mind is revealed.

Words can deceive, intentions can deceive. Actions do not deceive. When you look at your actions, then you come to see your real stuff.

When you can see who you are, then you know what you are working for. The one you are working for is not worth working for. Having seen his real face—oh, it resembles so much another face that we know of: our own.

Having seen the face of our employer, we no more want to work with him. One then really enters the service of the one who is worth serving, and that is called dedicating your actions to the Lord. That is *Bhakti*. That is *Karma Yoga*.

The right action is when the fruits of the action will dissolve you rather than continue you or strengthen you.

34

Action without Attachment Is Yoga

Myth Demolition Tour, Rishikesh, 2017

*Littleness would not come to you as littleness. It would
come to you as friendly advice, as brotherly concern, as
the sermons of a teacher, as a promise of security. To
be in Yoga is to refuse everything that keeps you little
and limited.*

~

योगस्थः कुरु कर्माणि सङ्गं त्यक्त्वा धनञ्जय ।
सिद्ध्यसिद्ध्योः समो भूत्वा समत्वं योग उच्यते ॥

*Perform your actions, O Dhananjaya (Arjuna) being
established in or integrated with Yoga, abandoning
attachment and remaining even minded both in success
and failure. This evenness of mind is called Yoga.*

—Shrimad Bhagavad Gita, Chapter 2, Verse 48

~

Questioner (Q): What does Yoga mean?
Acharya Prashant (AP): The science of uniting the
individual consciousness with the ultimate consciousness,
this equanimity, is known as Yoga.

Which equanimity is he talking of? Becoming equipoised
in success and failure. Could you get a more concise and

direct definition of Yoga? Perform your activities giving up attachment, and become equipoised in success and failure. This is Yoga.

What does it mean to remain equipoised in success and failure?

Q: To not become a football of situations and circumstances?
AP: It means that even when you enter an action, you enter it as somebody to whom the action does not matter too much. It is then not about the action but the actor. You enter as an already fulfilled actor: I am acting, but the actor is not acting for the sake of rewards; the actor is already fulfilled.

When the actor is already fulfilled, then the action does not matter too much; then one can have a little playfulness about the action. 'It does not matter which way the thing goes because whatever I wanted to have has been achieved even before the action; the action cannot really bring anything new to me. I am all right as I am. I am not acting in order to become all right.' This is Yoga. Too simple? *(Smiles)* Unbelievable?

This is the science of decision-making and acting. 'I am all right as I am. I am not acting to become all right, yet I am acting. Why am I acting? Just like that! I may as well not act and that would make no difference to my health. I may as well doubly act, with triple the intensity and energy, and that, too, would not really make a difference.' This is Yoga.

Now success and failure cannot really matter because they can neither inflate nor diminish you. Why won't they inflate you? 'Because I am already all right. What can the fruit of my action give me? I require no fruit.' Ah, wonderful word: I *require* no fruit. 'That doesn't mean that there would be no fruit; there would be fruit, of course. Each cause bears an effect; the tree would bear the fruit. But I *require* no fruit. If I get a fruit, wonderful. Nice fruit, nice taste! Ah, a little bitter? It is okay. I require no fruit. I am already all right.' This is Yoga.

To not have the thought that you are diseased is health, and that is Yoga. Yoga is not about feeling special. Yoga is not about being in a great state of consciousness. Yoga is about *not* having a lot of things that we usually have.

Now, what do we usually have? We usually have inferiority; we usually have lack of fulfillment; we usually have a lot of search and seeking; we usually have a lot of questions. Yoga is about not having these.

'I am already all right. What would I do with achievement? I am already all right. What would I do with medicines and methods? I am already all right. What would I do with questions and their answers?' That is Yoga.

Yoga is not a special feeling, mind you. Yoga is the absence of that which we usually keep feeling. Look at the common man on the road, look at the streets of Rishikesh. Do you see people with no feeling? No. People are walking, and they are walking with a lot of feeling. The feeling might be divine—so-called divine; it might be heavenly; it might be different from the feeling that one usually has in a metro city, in a corporate city. It is a holy city, so you have different feelings.

Yoga is to be free of all feelings. Yoga is to not place any demand on any kind of thought or feeling.

Every thought, every feeling arises as a promise, as a solution. It says, 'There is something missing in your life, I will provide that to you.' To be situated in Yoga is to not need any promises. 'I do not require your promise because whatever you would promise, I already have that. What can you promise to me when I have the Highest?'

Hence, Yoga is to be free of a lot of things. That does not mean that in Yoga you do not have those things; that does not mean that the yogi kills those things. Thoughts are still there, feelings are still there, yet there is freedom from thought and feeling.

We said cause would bear effect. We said action would bear fruit, so the fruit is still there. *Prakriti* operates, so the body is there. *Prakriti* operates, so thoughts are also there, but one does not place a lot of demands on thought; one does not want to think his way to wellness. Don't we use thought as a means to our welfare? When we are not well, what do we do? We think how to be well. Whenever we are faced with a problem, what do we do? We think how to get a solution.

In Yoga, you do not place the onus of your welfare upon anything or anybody simply because you are already well. In Yoga, you do not follow any path or any role. Why? Because you are already home.

Hence, Yoga is not at all about following this method or that method. Yoga is about realizing that all methods are futile. 'I am already there! I do not need any of these tactics.' If tactics are there, then one would want success from those tactics, and Krishna is saying, 'You have to be equanimous towards success and failure.' Hence, success is not something that you can take seriously.

Action without attachment is Yoga, and action without attachment is possible only when the actor is a very, very innocent and healthy actor; then he acts just for fun, just for no reason. Such acting has a beautiful quality about it because then it is not the action of a beggar.

When you are desirous of a result, you go about like a beggar who acts in order to get a result. Why does a beggar approach you? Does he approach you in love? He approaches you because he wants something from you. He wants a result. That is how the lot of mankind goes through life doing whatever it does for the sake of getting something. That is *viyoga* (disunion, separation).

Krishna is saying, 'No! Do not act to get. Realize that you already have it, and *then* act.' He is inverting the way we act. We act so that we may get. Krishna is saying, 'Get, and *then* act.'

And that is a little incomprehensible to our purpose-driven mind because we ask, 'If we have already got it, then why would we act at all?' You would know that when you are free of the thought that you do not have it. Then you will see what joy lies in acting even though you do not need the action.

We do not know the charm of needlessness. When you do something needlessly, reasonlessly, there is a particular beauty about it. That beauty is Yoga.

To live without a reason, to love without a cause, to act without greed and desire, that is Yoga.

Total purposelessness is Yoga. Yoga is freedom from all whys.

Yoga is freedom from all questions. Yoga is freedom from all concepts and theories and *sutras*.

Yoga is simply the statement: 'I am all right.' You need not say you are *Brahman*; you need not say you are God or the son of God or the daughter of God; you need not say you are the Ātmān; you need not say that you are the holy Truth. All you need to say is, 'I am not unwell.' I am not even saying that you need to say that you are all right because then even that would become a concept.

We are buffeted by the thoughts of not being well. In fact, every single thought that we have is a thought about our sickness. When everything is all right, do you think about it? When do you think about your thumb? When do you think about your tooth?

Q: When it hurts.

AP: When it hurts! Thought itself arises when there is a perception of something being problematic, of something being not all right. So, Yoga is simply freedom from thoughts of disease.

That does not mean that thoughts are not there, I am repeating this. Thoughts will be there, yet you will be free of them, you are not laying importance upon them. Thoughts are doing what they must, and you are where you must be. You are following your own nature, thoughts are following their own patterns, and you are not obliged to interfere in the patterns of thought or body. They are taking their own due course; you are letting them do what they want to do. This is Yoga.

Yoga means that you would not be unsettled by the fierce currents of body, mind, *Prakriti*, even as they flow all around you.

One of the most beautiful images of Yoga is the statue of Shiva in the middle of the Ganges. Have you seen that statue at Haridwar? The Ganges is flowing all around Shiva, and Shiva is still. That is Yoga.

The streams of *Prakriti* are flowing all around you, even over you, and yet they are not carrying you away. That is Yoga.

To be seated unflinchingly like Shiva is Yoga, which means that life goes on and does what it does, and you keep relaxing; you keep relaxing even as your body-mind apparatus keeps responding to life.

That does not mean that you have become lazy or incapable of right action. In fact, you are now capable of right and vigorous action, and yet you are relaxing.

With the Ganges all around you, you are relaxing like Shiva. That is Yoga. And in your relaxation lies the potency for vigorous action, right action. That is Yoga.

Yoga is giving up of all that which proves to you that you are little, inferior, handicapped, or small. To be in Yoga is to be with Krishna. To be with Krishna is to be *only* with Krishna and not with that which is sick, ugly, limited, and an agent of grief.

To be in Yoga is to not touch anything, anybody, any situation that causes a sense of littleness in you. Even if that littleness is induced in you in a holy pretext, even if it is induced in you as an ostensible means of welfare, you refuse to admit it in.

Somebody may come and say, 'You need protection!' You quickly see through what he is saying: you realize he is saying that you are weak. 'If I am not weak, why would I need protection?' You refuse to entertain the advice. You refuse to take that person seriously. This is Yoga.

Somebody comes and tells you, 'You need God and God is all that you need.' You refuse to entertain this person because if he is saying that you need God, then surely he means that you do not have God; he is proving that you are Godless. You refuse that person.

Somebody comes and says, 'You need a lot of self-enquiry.' You immediately refuse this person because if you need to look, see, and discover, then surely, first of all, you must believe that you do not know because you are ignorant, which you are not.

To be in Yoga is to refuse everything that keeps you little and limited.

Littleness would not come to you as littleness. It would come to you as friendly advice, as brotherly concern, as the sermons of a teacher, as a promise of security.

Had littleness been honest enough to admit its real name, you could've easily refused it. But littleness rarely admits its real name. Littleness comes wearing the mask of things that appear nice and sweet and promising.

Be very cautious of all this stuff that is always ready to enter your mind. Anything that promises to make you better is an allegation upon you. Why is it an allegation? It is an allegation that you are currently not all right.

Anybody who offers to improve your life or help you realize that which you do not know, is actually proving to you that ignorance is what you are. The advertiser who is telling you that the next home or the next position or the next car will add something to your life is actually causing *viyoga* in you because he is proving to you that unless you have that house or that car, there is something missing in life. And you buy into that. Why? Arjuna, too, must have bought into a lot of those things!

We do not know the charm of needlessness. When you do something needlessly, reasonlessly, there is a particular beauty about it. That beauty is Yoga.

To live without a reason, to love without a cause, to act without greed and desire, that is Yoga. Total purposelessness is Yoga. Yoga is freedom from all whys.

35

You, as the Doer, Are Unnecessary

Course in Realization, BodhSthal, 2018

It is not your doing that is needed. Hands know what to do, the speech knows what to do. You are an unnecessary intermediary.

~

अनादानविसर्गाभ्यामीषन्नास्ति क्रिया मुनेः ।
तदेकनिष्ठया नित्यं स्वाध्यासापनयं कुरु ॥

The sage has no connection whatsoever with action, as he has no accepting or giving up. Therefore, through constant engrossment on the Brahman alone, do away with thy superimposition.

—Vivekachudamani, Verse 282

~

Questioner (Q): What does it mean to have no connection with one's action? How do I apply that in my daily life? How does one come to a stage where there is no connection with action?
Acharya Prashant (AP): How are you connected to your actions? Go into that. Before we delve into not being connected with one's action, firstly let us understand what we call as remaining connected with one's action.

221

What kind of connection do we have with our action?
You do something. What is your relation with that action?
You want something from that, right? It must protect what
you consider as valuable, it must get more of what you think
as valuable, it must do away with something. There is always
an expectation attached with action. That is one's connection
with action.

You see, as I am speaking, my limbs are moving. Maybe
not my legs so much but certainly the hands, the arms.
Action is happening, right? What if I have an idea of what
the right action is like? What would happen to the quality of
my movement? How would that make me feel? How would
that affect my consciousness? If I have an idea of what the
right gestures are or what the right words are or what the right
way of looking at the audience is, if I have that relation, that
connection with my action, what would happen to this being?
How would I feel?

If you have an idea about what the right way of speaking at
this very instant is, in advance, what effect would it have upon
you?

Q: We won't be able to express.
AP: Why won't you be able to express? What if you knew
in advance what the right way of turning to him was? Right
now, your hands are like this *(gestures)*. What if he knew in
advance the right way of making your limbs act? And who
will be holding the responsibility to make it perfect?

Q: Me.
AP: You. How do you feel under that responsibility?

Q: Crushed.

AP: Crushed! And what if you have no responsibility to take care of what is happening? What if you have no responsibility to come up with perfect words or perfect movements of limbs? Then what is your relation with the hand, with the speech? They are free, and you are free.

Now, let the limbs do what they want to do, and let speech do what it wants to do. Remain distant.

Q: But still, we have fear of failure and society.

AP: What is failure?

Q: Getting a certain kind of a . . .

AP: So, if the hand goes this way *(moves hand in one direction)*, this is success, and if the hand goes this way *(moves hand in another direction)*, this is failure, right?

Success and failure are nothing but pre-programmed connections with the action. If the action happens one way, I call it a success. If the action happened some other way, I term it a failure.

Now, what is the verse saying? 'The sage has no connection whatsoever with action.' Action belongs to the actor. The actor is always the one who can move, the one who has no option but to move, to act. The bloodstream, the heart, the breath, the mind, the limbs—do they have an option not to move? They would necessarily . . .?

Q: Move?

AP: Is there a single atom in the entire universe that does not move? How many atoms are there in the universe? If you count them, you will get a taste of infinity. Then you will know that *Brahman* is not merely fiction; something called infinity does exist.

Out of all these atoms, show me one that is still. Physics would tell you that perfect stillness to an atom comes at zero kelvin (minus 273 degrees centigrade). Elementary physics tells you that zero kelvin has never been reached. Even to an atom, stillness never comes. Everything is always acting, and it requires no consciousness. Things just move because it is their *prakriti* (nature) to move.

There is nothing that can ever be still. Why are you attributing that movement to yourself? Even dead men move. Even dead men belch and fart. Would you say this fellow is doing it? Even after you are dead, your body keeps moving. What do you think, the moment you are gone, 'you' meaning the . . .

Q: The soul?

AP: . . . doer-consciousness—no, not soul. Even when the doer-consciousness is no more, the body is still moving. No atom of the body is going to lie still, ever. What is your role there and why are you needed there? Why do you think that it is your responsibility to control all the action? By taking that responsibility upon yourself, you have taken a massive load on your head. You are saying, 'I must dictate action.'

Doership is not about doing. Doership is about assuming that you are the doer.

Please differentiate between these two. It is not as if you give up doership and doing would cease. Doing is the *prakriti* of the Universe. Rather, action is the *prakriti* of the Universe. But the stupid self-starts assuming that he holds the responsibility to do and to do rightly. The fact of the matter is otherwise: the more you want to take matters into your hands, the more you trouble yourself. Without you things are so very right! It is not as if some great intervention from your part is needed.

Somebody asked me, 'How can man save the Earth? Poor Earth is withering away, going away.' I said, 'By not doing anything for the next ten years.'

You don't need to save the Earth; you just need to stop doing. Don't do anything for the next ten years, and Earth will be back to the pink of health. And if you want absolute health back, then let there be no intelligent activity for the next fifty years. Keep your intelligence aside, and everything will be all right again.

And by the way, the Earth is not sick. The Earth is just adjusting itself in a way that would eliminate human beings. The Earth will go nowhere; man will disappear. And once man is not there, the Earth is back to fine fettle. Several species who just go into hiding, if they remain at all, would again sprout forth. It is man, the weakest of all species, that would be eliminated.

It is not your doing that is needed. Hands know what to do, the speech knows what to do. You are an unnecessary intermediary. The speech knows from where to directly take orders, this hand also knows. Who are you? Who is talking about doing the action, being the actor?

The heart knows—the physical heart, that is—to take orders from *Prakriti*. Is your consciousness needed to make the heart beat? It knows to take orders for *Prakriti*. Because it is material, it knows where to take orders from. What if you start giving orders to the heart?

The intestines know from where to take orders. All the organs of the body know from where to take orders. They take orders directly from *Prakriti*, and it is best when they take orders *only* from *Prakriti*. Or would you rather want a pacemaker? If you have a pacemaker here in this hollow *(points to the heart)*, then your heart is taking orders from man, not from *Prakriti*. What would you prefer? A heart that takes orders from *Prakriti*, or a heart that takes orders from a pacemaker?

Q: *Prakriti*.

AP: But you are pleased when you announce that you have now invented a pacemaker that can take the place of the heart. It is not the body that is pleased, really. The body loves the *prakritik* heart, not the pacemaker.

Similarly, the voice, the intellect know where to take orders from. They will not take orders from *Prakriti*. The entire *antaḥkaran* (mind, inner mechanism) knows where to take orders from. And it doesn't take orders from *Prakriti*.

Who are you, the one who is talking of being the doer? You are neither *Prakriti* nor *Paramātman* (Supreme Self). Who are you? This system can take orders either from *Prakriti*, or from *Paramātman*. Who are you, the doer? Would you reveal your identity? Who are you?

You are not *Prakriti*, for sure, because you are not material, and you are not *Paramātman* because you are not totally immaterial. You are some intermediary. Show your face! From where have you come?

Neither are you just baby-like or animal-like, totally *prakritik*, nor are you divine. Who are you? Neither are you like a little kid who is nothing but *Prakriti*, nor are you pure, immaterial, divine light. Who are you?

You are some needless middleman. You have too many of them in India, don't you? When the work can be done directly, we still trust the middleman. The ego is that middleman.

To take care of the body, *Prakriti* is sufficient. To take care of your worldly movements, basic worldly existence, *Prakriti* is sufficient. The nose knows how to breathe; you don't have to teach it. The eyes know how to blink; you don't have to teach them. Doership is not needed. The mouth knows how to salivate; the stomach knows how to digest. And they take their orders from *Prakriti*.

And the Heart—I am not talking about the physical heart, I am talking of your essence—it knows love, it knows the right action, it knows devotion, it knows freedom. It does not have to be taught to value freedom. It takes its orders directly from God, not from *Prakriti*. *Prakriti* has nothing for freedom.

Let the physical heart obey Prakriti. Let the spiritual heart obey Paramātman. Your directions, your interventions, are not needed.

As I am speaking, I am breathing. For name's sake, am I breathing? Am I the doer of the breathing act? No. Who is the doer?

Q: *Prakriti.*

AP: And my job is to let *Prakriti* remain the doer. If I try to regulate my breathing, I will only distort it. And as I am speaking, these words are being regulated by Him. Am I the doer? My job is to firmly stand aside as an attendant; my job is to not interfere when the master is speaking. Just as you are listening to Acharya Prashant, I, too, am listening to Acharya Prashant. He is my master as well. My job is to not interfere when he speaks. My job is to not interfere with *Prakriti* when the breath goes in and comes out. My job is to not be the doer when somebody is speaking. Who is speaking? Not me! I am not the actor here.

You are so afraid and you are such a sucker for importance that you keep hanging around. You don't go away. You feel you are very important. You feel that if you go away, so many bad things will happen. No calamity is going befall you. In fact, if you go away, the real doer would find it far easier and smoother to act. You are just a hindrance.

Needlessly, one tries to be the doer. One is unnecessary. That which is necessary would anyway never go away. Have the guts to go away. Have the guts to acknowledge that you are not needed, you are unnecessary.

36

What Is Action, What Is Non-action?

Upanishad Samagam, BodhSthal, 2020

Doership is a foolish thing in two ways. First, you are not the doer; secondly, even if you claim to be the doer, it is extremely unlikely that the doing will satisfy you the way you expect.

~

किं कर्म ।

कर्मेति च क्रियमाणेन्द्रियैः कर्मण्यहं करोमीत्यध्यात्मनिष्ठतया कृतं कर्मैव कर्म ।

किमकर्म ।

अकर्मेति च कर्तृत्वभोक्तृत्वा-ऽहङ्कारतया बन्धरूपं जन्मादिकारणं नित्यनैमित्तिक्यागब्रततपोदानादिषु फलाभिसन्धानं यत्तदकर्म ।

What is deed?

'I do the deeds that are done through sense organs'—the deed thus done as centred in the self alone is the deed (in question).

What is a non-deed?

The deed done with conceit as agent and enjoyer,
causing birth, etc., binds; the non-deed is the obligatory
and occasional action, sacrifice, holy vow, austerity,
gifts, etc., done without desire for their fruit.
                        —Niralamba Upanishad, Verses 11, 12

Acharya Prashant (AP): Verses 11 and 12 pertain to the difference between karma (action) and *akarma* (non-action). It must be noted that karma, *akarma*, *vikarma*, and *niṣkāma-karma* have been covered in great detail in another Vedantic scripture, Shrimad Bhagavad Gita. So, we will obviously draw a lot from there because here in the Niralamba Upanishad, the whole matter confines itself to just one verse, rather two verses. We will draw from our understanding of the Bhagavad Gita.

What do the verses say? When you feel that 'I do the deeds that are done through the sense organs', the deed thus done is called karma, the deed, the doing, or the action. This is how the Upanishad defines karma. How does the Upanishad come to *akarma*? 'The non-deed is the obligatory and occasional action—sacrifice, austerity, gifts, etc.—done without desire for their fruit.' No, here the translation has missed out on something: done *with* desire for the fruit. However, that will not make much difference to the definition. We will go into that in detail.

So, what is action, karma? And what is *akarma*? Karma or doing or action is easier to understand. That with which you associate yourself as the doer is karma. Remember, you are not the doer; you are *associating* yourself with the action. Where is the action happening? The action is happening in the domain of the senses plus the mind—which in itself can be called an extended sense—but you start identifying with that action; you start calling that action as your property; you start owning it. In that sense, I am calling it a property.

You start taking responsibility for that action, and this responsibility is not really a virtue. You start taking ownership of that action because you are desirous of the fruit of the action. You know very well that if you want to consume the result of the action, you will, first of all, have to claim that you are the owner of the action. If you do not own a property, let's say a field, can you claim what grows on that field? Let's say, fruits and vegetables come up on that field. If you intend to consume them, then you should have, first of all, laid a claim to the very field itself: 'I own it.' Now, that's the reason why the misled, ignorant 'I'-sense claims the action. Otherwise, there is hardly any need.

Something is happening, now something will come out of it, right? These are just changing phenomenal states, cause-and-effect phenomena; something is happening, something will follow from that; like a stream of time, stream of cause and effect. This is happening, so something else results from that. Then there are so many things that all get together to proceed towards something else.

Now, first of all, we do not know what will come from what because the number of factors that get together to produce any outcome is simply innumerable. Secondly, we do not know in what particular way and to what effect will those factors combine, and yet we have a hope that they will combine in the way we desire. And what is our desire? Our desire is that they will combine in a way that produces a fruit that we have already known of in the past.

Let's say, you have tasted some particular sweet at some point in your life. Let's say, *barfi* (Indian sweetmeat). So, you have that pleasure of barfi stored in your memory. You do not exactly know what factors get together to ultimately give you a product like barfi. But the experience, that memory of barfi really overpowers you; you are captivated. You want that experience again, so you apply your intellect and you guess what all went into the making of barfi. You guess there was some sugar because you tasted it and it was sweet; probably, there was some milk; probably, there was some corn, some flour, something. So, you guess all these things, and now you want to see all these things come together in the hope that when they do, at the required temperature, in the required way, frozen for the right period of time, and all such things—and all of these phenomena, heat, pressure, temperature, ingredients, what are these? These are the worldly stuff. So, you want all these worldly things to get together as causes, hoping that their aggregation will give you the particular effect called barfi.

Now, wherever you see these things getting together or the possibility of them getting together, you start claiming that you are the one causing them to get together. You go to some place, for example, where a man seems to be gathering all these things—some grated coconut is there, some milk, some sugar—and that man is sitting and he has all this stuff. Now, the moment you look at him and all this stuff, what comes to you? 'These causes are there—now they will probably result in a barfi!' But you cannot have that barfi because it belongs to that man. If the man is actually the doer, then who will have claim over the product, the doing? That man.

Now, you see that in the next thirty minutes, probably, the barfi will result from all this accumulation, so what do you do immediately? You do something utterly dishonest: you lay claim on the happening.

This is called doership. This is karma. The actual doer is somebody else, but you have hopes from the doing. And what do you expect to result from the doing? Something that you have already experienced in the past.

Now it is a double deceit. Firstly, you are not the doer; secondly, you are fooling yourself by thinking that the process will result in exactly the same experience as the one you have had in the past. Do you really know what goes into the making of barfi? Had you really known that, what would you have done? You would have made it yourself. So, you really do not know; you are just shooting in the dark; it is a blind guess, just as we all guess and hope and pray that some positive outcome will result from our endeavours. Don't we do that? Are we ever certain? We are speculating and we are afraid, right?

So, doership is a foolish thing in two ways. First, you are not the doer; secondly, even if you claim to be the doer, it is extremely unlikely that the doing will satisfy you the way you expect.

There is a third and underlying deeper deceit as well. Can you help me with it? What is the fundamental deceit here? We have already talked of the two current deceits. One, you are not the doer; you are arbitrarily and dishonestly claiming to be the doer; you very well know that the doer is somebody else, that the event can happen without your intervention or presence. You know that. You disappear from the scene, and the cooking will still happen if the cooking is to happen at all. You do not even know why the man has aggregated all that stuff. Maybe he has no intention of producing any sweets. You do not know. And even if he has a particular intention, that intention in no way depends on you; you get lost, the thing will still happen.

So, that's the first level of dishonesty.

Second is: you are bluffing, first of all, to yourself; you do not know whether all this will result in the desired outcome.

I am asking for the deeper and underlying dishonesty.

Q: That it will satisfy me in the future?

AP: Go deeper than that. You are right, but then, why should you talk of the uncertain future? Has this not already happened with you once in the past? When? When you first savoured that barfi. Have you not had an experience already? So, what is the fundamental self-deceit?

Q: That it satisfied me the last time.

AP: Yes. It is on that assumption and self-deceit that you are basing all your future actions. You are telling yourself: 'The last time it happened to me, it was so great.' Was it? It wasn't great even in the past! How will it be great when the past is replicated in the future, if at all?

We want our future as some kind of replica of the past, right? Maybe exaggerated replicas, decorated replicas, face-lifted replicas. But no man can ever visualize a future that is fundamentally separated from his past. In fact, all visualization is an exercise in retrospect.

When you are visualizing, you feel as if you are looking ahead. The fact is that when you are visualizing, you indeed are looking ahead but just as a car driver looks ahead into the rear-view mirror. It appears as if the fellow is looking ahead of himself, but he is actually looking behind. That's what visualization is.

Visualization, therefore, can never give you anything really new, and that is the reason why all these self-help and motivational techniques based on visualization are bound to bomb. When you visualize, what do you want? A repetition of your already sorry and stale state. Look at your current state. How are you right now? If you are happy and all right, why would you want to visualize? Isn't self-help based on the premise that currently you are not okay? If you are not currently okay, is not your current situation a product of your past?

As the Ishavasya Upanishad says, '*Krato smara kṛtaṃ smara, krato smara kṛtaṃ smara*' (Remember the doer, remember the deed; remember the doer, remember the deed). Do you remember all your deeds? Remember what you have done. Your current situation is not without reason—*you* are responsible.

So, your past was really not that great; it resulted in the miserable thing you call your present. And what are you doing when you visualize? You are just trying to replicate that same past that has resulted in the current disaster called 'you'. Therefore, visualization can never be successful. If it is successful, it will be a bigger disaster.

Do you see the whole environment of doership? Doership involves choice, but it is semi-conscious choice. You are choosing, which is a good thing, but the whole purpose of consciousness is to choose discreetly. Discretion is missing. Choice is there, but it is indiscriminate choice. Instead of choosing something entirely new, you are just choosing to repeat the past. And what a shame it is that you are trying to repeat the past that never satisfied you in the first place!

Had the past been any good, had the past really been favourable to you, it would have been understandable that you want to relive your past, right? After all, the past was such a golden period, who won't want to live it? But that is not the case. Look at the absurdity, look at the absolute stupidity. The past was not great at all! The proof is that you still wallow in it; the proof is that it has resulted in a present that is not at all charming enough to hold you captivated. The good old days resulted in a condition in which you are continuously harking back to the so-called good old days. Now, were the good old days really good? Had they been really good, they would have liberated you of themselves. Do you get this?

Had the past been really good, then it would have resulted in a present in which there would be no need to go back to the past.

That's the mark of any auspicious thing. Its output is residueless and independent of itself; it leaves you free of itself. And what is the sign of anything that is inauspicious for you? It will blemish you; it will never leave you even after you want to leave it behind; it will scar you; it will stubbornly leave its traces upon your existence, your psyche. You will want to just brush it off, leave it behind, but you will find that it is clinging, it is sticky. This stickiness is a sure-shot sign of inauspiciousness.

Q: What is meant by indiscriminate choice?

AP: Indiscriminate choice is fundamentally dishonest choice. You are choosing against yourself; you are not being good to yourself; you are telling lies to yourself—as if one ever got anything by keeping himself in the dark. Who wants to guess why we do all this? I mean, if the past was not good, if the barfi was not really so delicious, why do you want to repeat the experience? Think, think! These are the questions that you should be asking.

Saṃkhyā (an Indian system of philosophy) explains it. *Saṃkhyā* says, 'Sir, all that you are saying right now is coming from a very elevated state of consciousness, but it is not always this way. You are not always merely the free and light consciousness that you are in this moment; at other times, you are what you are: the body.' Consciousness has no weight, but the body has weight. Pure consciousness is just light— it hardly has any inertia, it is feather-like—but the body has inertia. When the body has inertia, it has a certain laziness.

If you accept that the past was not really great, then you will have to redo, rework, create something new, and that involves effort, labour, and work. *Tamoguṇa* (quality of darkness, ignorance, laziness) doesn't allow that. The body doesn't allow that; the body has inertia. We do not live *sāttvika* (quality of purity, harmony, knowing) lives. Our systems carry a lot of momentum. When a system carries momentum, how easy is it to change its velocity? When you apply brakes to a bicycle, how soon does it stop? When you apply brakes to a passenger train, how soon does it stop? Unfortunately, we do not even live like a passenger train; we live like a freight train carrying a lot of baggage—so many people, so many things— and we carry all that. We are just too heavy. So, it is not easy to change direction; there is a lot of momentum.

When there is a lot of momentum, the force that is required to change direction is equally large: $F=dp/dt$. Such great momentum! From where will you muster the corresponding force? That force will then have to come from your commitment towards the Truth, your commitment towards liberation. Not everybody has that commitment; therefore, not everybody is able to summon the inner force needed to change the habits of the past.

Two things are there. First of all, your *tāmasika* inertia
has to be as low as possible; you should be carrying as little
mental weight as possible; the mind has to be very, very light,
like a feather. Secondly, practically, you know that some
weight will always be there because you are born a human;
practically, some baggage would always be there in the mind,
but you want to change direction. Having learnt that you are
not going in the right way, you quickly want to course-correct.
For that you must summon ātmabala (self-strength).

Now, this ātmabala is very different from willpower.
Ātmabala arises from the mind's love and devotion towards
its own welfare. That is what gives power to the mind. Mind
says, 'I might be moving towards the north, but I have just
learnt that my welfare is towards the south, so I will apply
the brakes.' And when a system carrying a lot of momentum
is braked suddenly, you know what happens? There is great
stress on that system; a lot of heat and noise is generated. You
should be prepared to take that. That is called sacrifice.

The brakes have been suddenly jammed, so much so that
the system can even catch fire. All the kinetic energy will have
to go somewhere. Where would it go? It would turn into heat,
sound, and so many other things. You have to be prepared
to let the system go to flames. You are saying, 'I am prepared
to turn to ashes, but I am not prepared to keep going north
when my welfare, my beloved, my liberation is to the south.
I fully well know that my body is carrying me towards the
north. I will not go in that direction.' It is the momentum, it
is the *tāmasika* inertia of the past. It is saying, 'Go, go, carry
on, carry on.' It is rolling, and you very well know that a
rolling object will keep rolling. Why would it stop on its own,
or would it? It won't. It wants to keep rolling. But you are

not that rolling object; you are somebody who is somehow, unfortunately, contained inside that rolling object but who is not that rolling object. That distinction is the basis of all spirituality. You are contained in that massive rolling object, but you are not that object.

So, you have discovered: 'I am not to go north,' and with all your might you say, 'This thing has to stop right now!' When you apply the brakes so very hard, then there are consequences. What do you say? 'I am prepared to take the consequences.' Now, this kind of action, you could simply call it *niṣkāma-karma*.

You could either fool yourself: 'All my life I have been rolling towards the north. Oh, it was so delightful! So, I will continue rolling towards the north.' You could either deceive yourself this way, or you could simply admit: 'The past has all been a waste, but the past is still so much upon me; the past has not been left behind. I see that I am constituted of the past; all my movements, all my urges, impulses, my feelings, my instincts, they all come from my past. They are very dominant.' That's the momentum of the past, right? 'But I won't give in. If the whole system has to crash, so be it.'

So, you see the difference between karma and *niṣkāma-karma* here? Ordinary karma would say the system must roll on just as it was rolling in the past. So, you will do things, but you will do things just to keep the roller on track, and that track leads to a past-like future. This is the normal action that we all engage in. We want to do things; we exercise the choice. You can imagine somebody sitting inside the roller and he has the choice—he does have his hands on the steering—and there is the accelerator, the brake, the clutch, the gear, all that is there. So, the choice is there. When you have your foot on the accelerator, then it is normal doing. You are just letting your momentum continue and express itself. What are you doing with this steering wheel? Just minor adjustments, very minor adjustments. You have no intention to take a U-turn, right? So, you are exercising a choice. It is not as if you are sitting doing nothing inside the roller; the choice is being exercised. Don't we all say, 'This is my choice, this is my choice'? The fact is that when you are choosing in the usual way, you are choosing very little; you are just letting the rolling happen.

What is *niṣkāma-karma*? Having known what is right, you do what is right and forget the consequences. This forgetfulness towards the consequences is called *niṣkāmta*. 'I do not care for the consequences at all.' This is called *niṣkāmta* or action without expectation. 'I will just do the right thing, and I will let the rightness of my action decide for me. If my action is right, how can the consequences be wrong? I may feel that the consequences are not suitable for me, but that would be my feeling, not the reality.'

How do you know whether something that has happened to you is right? Figure out the effect from where the cause has emanated. If the action is right, the result cannot be wrong.

You have no way of knowing directly whether the result is right or wrong. All that you can ever know is whether the centre of action was right.

So, you act and then you leave it to the rightness. Or you could say you act and you simply leave it; act and leave it. 'If the action is right, how can the result be wrong? So, I leave it.'

This is what Krishna means when he says, 'Your right, your *adhikar* is at most over the action. Forget the result.' What he is saying is not something ideal; it is actually the reality. It is something very practical. Can you ever have any handle over the results? Has anybody ever enjoyed that? But in our fancies, we keep assuming as if the results would be as per our expectations, and that leads to so much sorrow and disappointment. The much better option is just do what is right—full stop. 'What would happen next? I don't care!'

Now, we come to *akarma*. In the entire translation, one word that you should underscore is 'obligatory'. In karma, in normal action, you feel you have a choice. In *akarma*, you feel you have no choice at all, rather you are acting out of compulsion, obligation. You have convinced yourself that this is something I have no control over, so you do not even attempt to navigate your ruler properly when it comes to these actions; you have just surrendered yourself to something called fate. You have said, 'This is something that necessarily happens. What do I do about it?' That is *akarma*.

Now, even this *akarma* can be of two kinds. First is *akarma* of the physical kind. Actions like breathing, digestion, blinking, growth of body, discharge of bodily fluids, movements of internal organs—these are things that you really cannot have much control over. You can play tricks with your heart and alter your heart rate. You can probably go out and run and you will find that your heart rate has increased. So, that much you can do but you cannot really order your heart to stop beating. Same with perspiration: You can probably control the rate of perspiration, but at no point can you reduce it to zero; some amount of perspiration is always happening. For how long can you control the blinking of your eyes? How much control can you have over your digestive juices?

So, this is *akarma* of the physical kind to which not much attention should be paid. These things happen, though occasionally it may be required to pay attention even to these things.

Then, there is the more severe kind of *akarma* that pertains to actions in which a mental choice is available, but we have convinced ourselves of our helplessness. We say, 'Oh, but I have no choice! I am optionless!' It is a fake and artificial helplessness.

Do you see the examples given here? Somebody has convinced you that such and such religious rituals are very necessary, and you go on performing those rituals all your life, telling yourself that these rituals are almost like heartbeat, like lunch and breakfast. Just as one eats daily, similarly one has to do all these things daily. You have convinced yourself and thereby you have given up your choice. Spiritual practice is about regaining your choice. These things that you are doing, these things that you feel so helpless in front of, are they really compulsory? Must you really kneel down in front of them?

For example, people of a particular cult or religious denomination feeling that they must kill animals—is that really obligatory? People of a certain age feeling that they must marry—is that really obligatory? In all these matters we just relinquish choice. We feel that these things are not alterable.

Only the Truth is not alterable. Do not raise social or even religious practices to the level of Truth.

Except for the Truth, everything is subject to conscious choice. There is nothing that cannot be decided upon; there is nothing that cannot be rejected; and equally, there is nothing that cannot be attempted and accepted.

So, *akarma*, in that sense, is a way of acting lower than even misguided or unconscious karma. In karma, you at least feel that you are on the driver's seat. In *akarma*, you feel that the driver is somebody else and you are just a hapless passenger being carried away in the vehicle of fate. And it is not something limited only to those who follow religious practices or those who live very social lives. Every time you say you are helpless against something, you are just displaying *akarma*.

None of us is ever helpless. Never say, 'What else could I have done?'

There is always something else that you could have done. There is always the right thing that you could have done.

All powerlessness is just a pretence. Even in your feeblest moment, you are still powerful enough to exercise choice, and you must always hold this very close to your heart.

The world can take anything, everything away from you, but nothing and nobody can ever take away from you your power to choose. That right has not been given to you by man; therefore, man cannot deprive you of that right. It is an existential right—the right to choose.

Those who say, 'What do I do? I am helpless!' are in the lowest state. They are the worst self-deceivers. They harm themselves and they pollute the entire environment.

A little better than these are those who at least try exercising choice, though their choices are all in the wrong direction.

The highest one is the one who knows what is right and chooses only in one direction. His choices, in fact, have all already been made. In some sense, his life is just a continuous reiteration of his one unchangeable choice. Every time he is asked to choose, he just repeats his one choice—though in many names, in many forms, in many languages. But whatever he says, whatever he chooses, fundamentally he is choosing just one thing.

That's our man. All this so that such possibility may inspire us. It is real, it is there for us to take. We are not looking at it or listening to it as some kind of fairy tale. We are looking at it so that we may be awakened to our own possibility, so that we, too, discover that we have the guts, the gumption to choose with abandon.

These are, if taken in the right sense, some of the holiest words: 'I don't care.' But, obviously, they have to be put in the right context.

All powerlessness is just a pretense. Even in your feeblest moment, you are still powerful enough to exercise choice, and you must always hold this very close to your heart.

37

Doership Is Bondage

Upanishad Samagam, BodhSthal, 2020

*Doership is necessitated by our incapacity, our poverty—
inner poverty, that is—and our inner disease, and
hollowness. That is what necessitates doership. If you
are not feeling all right, you will have to do something—
that's doership. The liberated one indeed does appear to
act, but he is not forced to act. His actions are sovereign.*

~

कर्तृत्वाद्यहङ्कारसङ्कल्पो बन्धः ।

*Bondage is the conceit of egoistic agency in regard to
actions, etc.*

—Niralamba Upanishad, Verse 20

~

Acharya Prashant (AP): How is doership related to body-identification? It is very important to understand this fundamental question. If you can appreciate it, you will never be misled.

When you are identified with the body, you are identified with a bundle of crying needs. Remember, the body has its needs—consciousness, too, has its needs—but they are diverse and unending. Even in the last moment of your life, you still require air to breathe, right? It might be your last moment, but you still need air. The needs of the body continue till death—and these needs are not at all deep. Shallow, but very widespread needs. 'I want this! I want this!' Little things. Little but endless.

Much in contrast are the needs of consciousness. Consciousness has just one need actually: liberation, and it is a very deep need.

You could take the needs of the body as the entire x-y plane. What is the area of the x-y plane? Infinite. But the x-y plane has neither height nor depth; it has no existence in the z domain. It is just a flat plane—flat and infinite. That's how the needs of the body are. Do you have a count of the number of clothes you have used so far in life? That's how numerous our basic demands are. Every time you inhale, do you know the number of molecules you take in? How much is one mole? Ten to the power . . .? Just keep counting the number of zeroes. With each breath, this is the number of those little things that you need—with each breath! The entire x-y plane is littered with your unending needs.

And what is the need of consciousness? It is not a plane; it is the z-axis. It has no area at all. It just has an ambition: want to reach, reach, reach, and reach there, or want to go deep, deep and deeper than anything.

There is an infinity in the plane and in the axis. It's just that when you choose to serve the needs of consciousness rather than the needs of body, you find that the needs of consciousness can come to an end. Even though the axis is infinite, that infinity is somehow attainable. It is a strange thing we are coming to.

That which you call as liberation or Truth—or in the usual language, God—can somehow be attained. The height of the z-axis can somehow come to a conclusion. That conclusion is called liberation. But the needs of the body are truly unending. If they are to end, the body will have to end. Otherwise, they are unending.

So, what does common sense say? Which need do you seek to fulfil, then? The one that is actually unending, or the one that can somehow be met and, therefore, ended?

Also, remember that even if you meet the needs of the body to a great extent, the unmet need of the z-axis will keep crying; whereas the higher you go up the z-axis, the more distance you have created from the x-y plane. Therefore, the needs of the x-y plane will no more be relevant to you. The needs are all there at ground level, the x-y plane, and where are you now? At a distance of forty light years. So, what is happening on the x-y plane doesn't really concern you.

The x-y plane, yes, it is still clamouring, 'Give me a little more food! Can I have one more t-shirt? Can I get a haircut please? There is a new brand of toothbrush in the market! The neighbours have just moved in and the woman is very attractive!' All these things, that regular melodrama is taking place. And where are you? *(Points upwards)* You can't even really see what is happening from up there. 'Those things are happening—I am on a spaceship.' That is spirituality. 'Things are happening on the earth—I am on a spaceship.'

What is happening on Earth? There is a volcano—it is a volcanic eruption! There is a nuclear war! Your wife or your husband ran away with someone! Where are you? *(Points upwards)* You don't even know! And even if you do know, you just peep downwards and say, 'All that is happening on that speck of dust called the planet Earth. It doesn't bother me. I go up, up, and up.'

Or you could be a scavenger on the x-y plane. What are you doing all the time? Scavenging: 'Can I get some food here?' and poking into waste food baskets as cows and dogs do. Always looking for something to ingratiate you, and always managing to find something or the other, and yet never feeling fulfilled.

However, do remember that for the spaceship to be launched, first of all, you require a launch pad on that same x-y plane. So, that x-y plane is not useless. And now you know what rightful use of the body is. What is the x-y plane all about? It is the dimension of the body. What do you use that x-y plane for?

Q: Launch pad?

AP: No, not even a launch pad. You, first of all, need a spaceship. Use the x-y plane to create a spaceship and a space station. The launch pad is there, you need a space station, too, maybe for various kinds of needs, such as refuelling.

Are all these pointers somehow enabling us to see what life is all about, and how do we make use of all these years that we supposedly have left? Are you able to see all that? Otherwise, they are just words. No Upanishad can benefit you if you do not see how it relates to your daily life.

Then comes doership. Doership is necessitated by the feeling of incompleteness, 'I am not okay, I will have to do something.'

Now, it is strange because we take pride in our doership, whereas the stark fact is that doership is necessitated by our incapacity, our poverty—inner poverty, that is—and our inner disease, and hollowness. If you are not feeling all right, you will have to do something—that's doership.

So, it is not so much about the statement 'I am the doer'. Honestly, the statement should be: 'I am *forced* to be the doer.'

A rabid dog is chasing you, a rabid dog is hot on your heels. Would you say, 'I am the runner,' and gladly click selfies and broadcast them, and have an app that measures speed and duration, and declare to the entire world how swift you are?

You are not the runner; you have been *forced* to run. That's what doership is about. That which you call as life is a rabid dog. It keeps chasing you all the time. And what are you doing? Running.

The Upanishad says this is bondage. Your actions are not yours; you have been forced to act. The liberated one indeed does appear to act, but he is not forced to act. His actions are sovereign. There is a difference between jogging for fun and running to save your backside, right?

However, it has been observed that those who run to preserve their behinds often set great records in running. In fact, all the great records belong to the ones who are running to save their backsides, and such people have inspired generations after generations of wannabe runners. And when you know that the only way to set a record is to have a rabid dog chasing you, then it becomes necessary to invent or manufacture rabid dogs.

That's the question you must ask: 'Am I acting or am I being forced to act?' And whenever you do something per force, I don't suppose you would want to call it freedom. If you say you are acting on your own, then ask yourself an innocent question: Do you even have the choice to not act? If you don't, then you probably have freedom.

Choicelessness comes in only two conditions: either there is a dog behind you—you are choiceless in the matter, you will have to run—or you are liberated. When you are liberated, again there is choicelessness because you are doing the one and the only thing that ought to be done. In your internal existence, you have no more options available. Now you are one internally, therefore, in your external world also, there are no more options left. Internally one, externally one, no choices anywhere. But that is a rare case. Most people do not have choices just because slaves do not have choices, just because beggars cannot be choosers.

Just for fun, sometimes ask yourself: What if I do not do this? There might be something that you supposedly do for your own sake. There might be something that you claim to do in love, right? You have a very loving person in your life. Most of us have these kinds of illusions at some time or the other. So, let's say you have a very loving person in your life, and there is something that you have to do for him or her. I said, just for fun, ask yourself, 'What if I do not do this?' And if the moment you ask this question a chill rises up your spine, you should know that there is a problem.

You are not doing this out of your freedom or love. Now you are a slave—a slave probably not to a scary monster but to a seductive princess, but nevertheless a slave. A slave is a slave. How does the slave-driver matter? The slave-driver could be monstrous or seductive. The moment you think about disobeying, if a warning rings in your ears, 'How dare you!' then you should know the fact of your life. Even before you have committed the act, the warning is already ringing—and what does it say? 'How dare you!'

You know where you stand. That is where most of our actions come from. You want to stop and something or somebody shrieks in your ears, 'How dare you!' and, therefore, you cannot stop; you will have to keep running. That is called doership. Rest is your natural state, but you cannot be at rest because you are terrified. So, you keep running.

'How dare you stop!' That's doership. And, therefore, the scriptures scoff at doership.

Somebody has been put in a jail, and there he is asked to grind cereals. I don't know what they do these days. From the olden days, we read that the inmates had to do such things. So, there are these things that he does for ten years. And after ten years, he is paid some money at the time of his release, and proudly he declares, 'This is what I have earned!'

Have you earned this? Technically, yes. But really? No.

For ten years the fellow was whipped into labour. He was whipped to work. And if he would refuse, then the sound of whiplashes would resonate in his ears. Imagine, whiplashes are reverberating. And then, at the time of his release, he proudly counts the money and says, 'Look, this is the great output of my blood and sweat!' Did you really do it? Technically, yes. Really, no.

That is how we live. We work a lot because we are so afraid that we will have to work. Rare is the one who works because work is his joy, work is fun.

'What else will I do if I will not work?'

Is there somebody pressurizing you to work? Do you work because you have to report to somebody? Do you work because if you do not report in time you will be scolded?

'No. I work because this is my personal joy. I don't work for somebody, I just work. I don't work for a reason, I just work. I don't work for a reward, I just work.'

Rare is this person. And such an individual is free of all doership, though he might appear to be engaged in intense work.

Work is something that the human condition cannot avoid. We work. Animals don't work. No animal ever works; they just exist. Horses are galloping, cows are grazing, lions are chasing—you don't call that work. Unless you domesticate an animal and subject it to slavery, animals don't work. Birds are chirping, that is not work. Rabbits are running around, that is not work. Though a lot of action is there, that is not work. Man is the only creature that works.

You have to figure out where your work is coming from. Is your work coming from fear? Or is your work your joy? These are two very, very different things. And when your work is coming from fear, it is called doership.

So, doership is nothing to be proud of. Never utter in your conceit, 'I did that!' You didn't do that. You had no option but to do that. You were pushed to do that.

See whether you can be somebody within who can find joyful work outside. I assure you, remaining who you are, you will find work that reflects your inner mess. Your insides and your outsides always carry a symmetry. The way you are within is the way you are without. The kind of work that you do in the world is indicative of something very important within you.

So, I am not asking you to go and find great work; I am asking you to be great within. If you are great within, obviously you will be doing great work. And if you are not great within, even if coincidently you chance upon great work, you will be a misfit. You will either spoil the work, or you will quit, or you will be thrown out.

So, you have to start from within. Be in a way that great work comes rushing to you. Just as water comes rushing to the right levels, to the right places. Have you seen how that happens after the rains? Water doesn't settle everywhere. It settles only at the right places. And right places need not necessarily be the low places. Many conditions have to be satisfied.

One thing is certain: water will not settle at conceited peaks. The ones who think too much of themselves will remain dry.

Remaining who you are, you will find work that reflects your inner mess. Your insides and your outsides always carry a symmetry. The way you are within is the way you are without. The kind of work that you do in the world is indicative of something very important within you.

38

Live Long Enough to
Reach the Right Place

Upanishad Samagam, BodhSthal, 2020

For the mind there never is fullness. In the world of the mind there always is discontent, dissatisfaction. A continuous lack of fulfilment is the mind.

~

ॐ पूर्णमदः पूर्णमिदं पूर्णात्पूर्णमुदच्यते ।
पूर्णस्य पूर्णमादाय पूर्णमेवावशिष्यते ॥

ॐ शान्तिः शान्तिः शान्तिः ॥

Aum! This is full; that is full. Fullness comes forth from fullness.

Even if fullness is taken from fullness, fullness remains. Aum! Shanti, shanti, shanti.

—Ishavasya Upanishad, Shanti Path

~

Questioner (Q): Clearly, the opening of the Upanishad itself is mysterious. Kindly say something.
Acharya Prashant (AP): You can call it mystery, or you can call it an exalted, bold, uninhibited expression of your deepest desire.

Who is the one going to this verse? To whom are these verses addressed? This question is very important. Otherwise, the verses would never disclose their meaning.

The word 'Upanishad' itself means the event that happens in nearness, proximity. That which happens when there is intimacy is called an Upanishad. Who is the one seeking intimacy? And with whom? It is the mind. You could call it the man, the woman, the person, but to be more precise, it is the mind that is seeking knowledge, relief, peace, light; it is the mind that stands to receive all these verses, this knowledge.

So, these verses are addressed to the mind. The mind is seeking the nearness of freedom or clarity or Truth. The phenomenon, the happening, in which the mind is coming close to the Truth is called an Upanishad.

In the world of the mind there always is discontent, dissatisfaction. A continuous lack of fulfillment is the mind. For the mind there never is fullness. And then, the mind is being told, 'This is full; that is full.'

Now, this is totally against the principle and experience of the mind. It is totally something new because the mind has never seen such a thing happening.

'This is full; that is full.'

The mind says, 'But I have never seen any fullness!'

But the words are coming from an authority, from the teacher. The mind has to listen; the mind has to receive. And the mind is being told, 'This is full; that is full.' It is something very novel, something very path-breaking, something extremely out of the mind's box.

First of all, fullness is a stranger to the mind. Secondly, all-pervasive fullness is not even imaginable. At most, the mind can come to agree that something has attained a bit of fullness, but here what is being said is that *everything* is full.

When it is said, 'This is full; that is full,' that does not merely indicate two things. You may as well envision the Rishi indicating with a fluent sweep of his hand, and the students sitting right in front of him, and him saying, 'This is full; that is full.'

If you have to refer to a thousand things, two are sufficient. Two indicates duality. The entire world is duality, so if you want to refer to the entire world, you just have to say, 'This is full; that is full,' meaning *everything* is full.

Now, the mind just cannot believe this; it is so much beyond any credulity. But somehow the student keeps sitting.

And then it is said, 'Fullness comes forth from fullness.'

Here you have something important; the student is getting some kind of a hint. 'So, fullness comes forth from fullness. If I cannot see fullness all around me, is it because I do not have fullness within?' So, even before the verses formally begin, the student has been delivered a lesson in humility.

The student is being told, 'You are looking for the Truth, so you are saying you haven't had the Truth so far. But then, fullness comes forth *only* from fullness. If you do not have fullness, then is it any surprise that you never see fullness anywhere around you, within you?' And the student is now getting introspective: 'Yes . . .'

So, the Upanishadic wisdom is not going to talk about something of the outside. If fullness can come only from fullness, then to obtain fullness I have to, first of all, go to myself. I have to dive deep within.

And then comes the concluding blow:

'Take away fullness from fullness and what remains is still full.'

Now, this is totally beyond any experience or idea or imagination of the mind. What they are saying is: everything has been taken away and *still* everything remains.

Now, the student has never seen anything like this happening, but if the teacher is to be believed, then the student will have to disbelieve all his experiences and concepts—and that is exactly what the teacher wants. And the student is ready for it because fullness being taken away or even a part being taken away is never a welcome experience. Forget about everything being taken away from you; even if *something* is taken away from you, do you like it? And it remains a constant fear with everybody. 'What if this thing or that thing or everything gets lost?'

And here the teacher says, 'Even if everything gets lost, everything will remain with you provided you have that "everything" called fullness.'

So, the student's mind is being attacked and consoled doubly. First of all, the mind is being delivered a koan-like blow, and when that happens the mind comes to a standstill. The usual, regular, habituated movement of the mind comes to a stop as if the emergency brakes have been slammed. 'What? What did you just say? Fullness taken away from fullness, fullness still remains?'

Now, it is so very jarring, so extremely contrary to all that we call as common wisdom or usual experience, that the student just cannot take these words casually. The student will have to pay attention. The teacher has said something so unbelievable that the student just cannot let it pass.

So, the student is brought into deep attention. And when he pays attention to these words, he finds that there is peace beyond the initial feeling of shock. Because if nothing is to be lost even if everything is lost, then why should one worry? Then there is no need to be anxious or afraid. And fear is the root problem that all spiritual literature or education seeks to remedy.

Here, you see, even if everything is taken away from you, everything still remains *provided* you have everything. It is not being said that if fullness is being taken away from a part, fullness would still remain. For fullness to remain unconditionally with you, first of all you must have fullness. If you have fullness, then you cannot lose it. If you do not have it, then there is no need for someone to even take it away from you because you anyway do not have it. And if you have it, then it is unconditionally yours.

Can you imagine the kind of peace and security fullness brings to the mind? It is in the dire need of such security that the student has, first of all, gone to the teacher. And the teacher has actually said whatever he has to say in the opening verse (*Shanti Path*) itself. The teacher must be inwardly smiling because the complete answer has already been given. No other Upanishad is needed, not even the rest of the Ishavasya Upanishad. Everything is contained in the Shanti Path itself. The teacher has already delivered everything.

Now, whatever the teacher will say here onwards will just be an elaboration or an elucidation. And this need to make things more lucid to the student is only there because the student is still not up to it. Had there been a more capable student, there was no need to elucidate.

That's the thing with teachers. They listen to the question or they look at the student, and they know what the matter is. And often the entire reply or the entire solution is contained in the first sentence of their answer, but it is quite possible that they may go on and speak for another twenty minutes, or they may go on and write an entire book to explain things to the questioner.

But remember, the teacher does not really need so many words or so much time or so much space to give the answer. The answer has been delivered in the first sentence itself. And sometimes there have been students who have been so ripe and so ready that the teacher just hints at the answer and the student says, 'I got it.' But those students are rare, so the teacher has to speak a lot often.

If you have fullness, then you cannot lose it. If you do not have it, then there is no need for someone to even take it away from you because you anyway do not have it.

39

How to Decide How Much to Consume

Upanishad Samagam, BodhSthal, 2020

Anything that you will ever run after is actually arising from within you, in a way to bring you back to yourself.

~

ईशा वास्यमिदं सर्वं यत्किञ्च जगत्यां जगत् ।
तेन त्यक्तेन भुञ्जीथा मा गृधः कस्यस्विद्धनम् ॥

All this, everything that moves in this moving world, must be pervaded by the Lord. Enjoy what has been renounced. Do not covet anyone's wealth.

—Ishavasya Upanishad, Verse 1

~

Acharya Prashant (AP): This is probably one of the most famous and most mysterious verses in the Upanishadic treasure. There have been a lot of people who have spoken on it, and Mahatma Gandhi used to say that if he were to forget all the spiritual reading he had done and he could just remember the first verse of the Ishavasya Upanishad, it would be sufficient. *Īśā vāsyamidam̐ sarvam*—these words were very dear to him. And there have been many luminaries who have loved this verse.

'All this, everything that moves in this moving world, must be pervaded by the Lord.' It is this verse that lends the Upanishad its name, Ishavasya. 'Enjoy what has been renounced. Do not covet anybody's wealth.'

Q: The first verse is imploring us to consume with renunciation. What does that imply?

AP: So, if you look at the basic Upanishadic principles, the Upanishads concern themselves with *Brahman*, the ultimate Truth, the Reality. Therefore, education in Upanishads is called *Brahmavidya*. Not *Isavidya*, *Brahmavidya*.

The Upanishads aren't really too fond of Īśvara, but this opening verse refers to Īśvara. And, strangely enough, after this verse Īśvara is not mentioned again in the entire Upanishad. So, it has to be interpreted considering the overall environment and thrust and philosophy of the Upanishads. The Upanishad here is referring to *Saguna Brahman* (the qualified Absolute). Īśvara or *Īśa* here is *Brahman*, *Brahman* that can be talked of. Hence, *Īśa*.

And the Upanishad says, '*Īśā vāsyamidam' sarvam*.' All this that you see is actually pervaded by the Truth. Truth is within it, Truth is without it. Truth is at the centre of all this that you see, and Truth envelops all this that you see.

Īśā vāsyamidam' sarvam. If the Truth and only the Truth is within-without, then that leaves the student with an existential problem: 'Where am I?' If only the Truth is here, there, internally, externally, then that leaves no space for even the student.

And the student is wondering, 'Sir, please? A little quarter? A few inches for me to remain and survive and question?' No. You are not permitted. 'But sir, if I am not permitted, how will I even listen to your discourse?' the student, the ego in audience pleads, resists.

And then the teacher says, 'All right, you can exist. But take only that much which has been given to you. Do not consume as per your likes, dislikes or inclinations or desires.'

Tena tyaktena bhuñjīthā. Now, this does not mean 'consume with renunciation' or 'consume with discretion'. Often it has been greatly misinterpreted. People have tried to justify their instincts to consume using this verse. They say that Ishavasya Upanishad recommends consumption with moderation. They say that '*tena tyaktena bhuñjīthā*' actually means that you should consume but with a certain degree of discretion, moderation, renunciation. No, that is not what is being said here. That is not even the formal meaning of the Sanskrit words.

The words '*tena tyaktena bhuñjīthā*' mean: Consume what has been given to you by the *Īśa. Tena tyaktena*—you get what He has renounced. What He has renounced, you take only that much. It has not been said that you consume with renunciation.

Tena tyaktena. What He has renounced, which means what He has given to you, what He has renounced—meaning what He has handed over to you—that kind of a given thing you can take and consume, but only that much.

Then it says, '*Mā gṛdhaḥ.*' Do not be greedy. In other words, at the beginning itself the student is being instructed not to be desirous. The teacher is telling the most fundamental things. 'You have come to me, son, and if you have come to me with your own desire or greed, you will not survive. If you have come to me, then things cannot proceed as per your wishes or your agenda, your wish list. You will have to listen.'

Then, 'Do not covet anybody's wealth.' The original Sanskrit here means, 'To whom does wealth belong?' which basically implies: do not covet anybody's wealth. Wealth anyway does not belong to you. If only the Truth pervades the entire expanse of consciousness, then whatsoever is in consciousness actually belongs to the Truth and not you.

What is this world? This world is the expanse of your consciousness. And the teacher is instructing the student that every bit of consciousness is permeated by, pervaded by the Truth. If you do not look carefully, you will probably think that the contents of consciousness are an objective reality by themselves. They are not. Truth is the root of the tree of consciousness.

What's more, Truth is the very sap rising through the trunk of that tree, sitting in the leaves of that tree, expressing itself as the aroma of the flowers of the tree and as the juice of the fruits of the tree.

So, Truth pervades the tree of consciousness in every way possible. It's just that when you do not bother to inquire into the insides and glance superficially only from the outside, then you will never find any sap in the tree. Neither will you see the roots, nor will you see the sap.

Looking at a tree, do you ever see the roots? No, the roots are invisible. Then, the roots send up the life-giving sap into the tree. Is the sap even visible from outside? No. Truth is the root and the sap. And remember that every bit of the trunk, the twigs, the leaves, the fruits, the flowers, is actually nothing but the sap. Without the sap, can there be the leaf? And how does a leaf grow in size? It is the sap that is becoming the leaf, is it not? It is the invisible sap that is becoming the visible leaf and growing in size and gaining some appearance.

So, you may look at the leaves and feel like calling them real and devoid of any internal truth. But all that is quite ignorant of you, is it not? So, all elements of consciousness have Truth at their centre and, therefore, belong to the Truth.

What is money? When money is being mentioned, you could interpret it broadly as an object of desire, right? What is money? An object of desire. In other words, all objects of desire can be theoretically called as money. So, the Upanishad is referring to *dhana* here. *Dhana* does not necessarily mean cash or currency or assets of some form. *Dhana*, in the context of the Upanishad, means any object of your desire. *Any* object of your desire.

All objects of your desire belong to the world, right? And the world really belongs to the Truth, its core element. Then why are you coveting? Who are you to desire so much? *Mā grdhah*. Don't desire so much, don't ask so much from life. You are nobody to ask. You are nobody at all! When you don't even exist, who are you to desire so much? But by desiring so much, you convince yourself that you do exist.

That is the inverted logic that we use. We say, 'If I am desiring so much, and also at least intermittently achieving something, then surely I do exist, don't I?'

The teacher is saying, 'No, no, no, no.' As we begin the Upanishad, we have to accept the absolute authority of the Truth. 'Son, it all belongs to something beyond your imagination. The Truth of it all is invisible to you and does not include the world of your fancies. The world of your fancies is quite unreal. Do not be so attached to it. Do not be so inclined towards what you have developed a fondness for.'

So, that's what the opening verse is about. The opening verse is a declaration of the absolute authority of the one thing that the student desires so much. And if that one thing is all-pervasive, omnipresent, and omnipotent, then the student's wishes have been answered, but his existence has been negated. The student's wish was to come to know that which is real; that wish has been answered. But in answering that wish, the existence of the wishful one has been negated.

So, the student was asking, 'What is the Truth?' The teacher has said, 'The Truth is that which is within everything, outside everything, which *is* everything.'

Now the student has been fully satisfied. But the student meditates a little more upon the teacher's answer, and what does the student realize?

'Well, my query has been satisfied, but by telling me that I don't exist, only the Truth exists. So, I am satisfied, but I do not exist anymore to enjoy my satisfaction.'

And that is quite a deep satisfaction, is it not? Because even to exist to enjoy satisfaction is a kind of a task. It is a burden, it is some kind of tension, is it not? You are being relieved even from experiencing enjoyment. Such total and deep relief!

Īśā vāsyamidam sarvam. Whatsoever you are looking at is in the field of consciousness. Without the conscious one, the world that you consciously experience does not exist. And this entire world that you see around you, that you project around yourself, exists for you only so that you may find the stuff of your desire in it.

Why do we project this entire universe? So that we have a great and expansive opportunity to hunt for something in it, right? Let's say, if your universe is very small, a small room, you will feel that the probability of finding something very rich, very fulfilling in your little universe is quite small, no? And the thing that you are looking for is really a behemoth. You are looking for something really huge because small things have anyway failed to satisfy you. And if there is something incredibly large that you are looking for to feel contented, then obviously you need a large universe in which that thing could probably be hiding and where you can go looking for it.

That is the reason why this entire universe exists for you. Don't we say the universe is infinite? Why is that? Because your desires are infinite. Let's say, you have big desires, and the universe is, as we said, just as small as a little room. Then can your desires ever be fulfilled? No. So, to support your infinite desires, what you require is a gigantic universe. That's why the universe is so large. And what is the universe? The expanse of your consciousness.

The seer is telling the student, 'This entire universe, son, you have mischievously created just because you are looking for something, and that which you are looking for is at the source of the consciousness that projects this universe.'

Consciousness is at best the trunk from where all the leaves and the flowers and fruits arise. Beneath the trunk is something more fundamental, though invisible, and that is the Truth.

You want the Truth. There is no need to wander so much among the leaves. The leaves are infinite. How many of them will you keep counting? Far better it is to go where your senses do not really advise you to go.

When you look at a tree, do you ever instinctively feel like exploring its roots? You don't. When you look at a tree, especially if the tree is laden with luscious fruit, what is it that you instinctively look at? The fruit. What is it that you immediately desire? The fruit. You don't even think of the root, or do you? We totally forget that the juice in the fruit is nothing but the root in action. But even the thought of the root does not come to us, or does it? Never.

That's what the teacher is saying. The root pervades the fruit: *Īśā vāsyamidam' sarvam'.* The *Īśā* is the root. '*Sarvam'* refers to this entire expanse of your universe, which is the tree of consciousness.

Before you get totally drunk upon the universe, remember that that which makes the universe comes from the root. And it is far easier to go to the root because it is within, much more accessible, much more intimate, and the universe is all external, outside. You can keep running all your life, and the universe will not come to an end. So, what is easier?

You can imagine a tree with its roots in your heart and its expanse outside of you, and it is so expansive that it occupies the entire universe. Can you imagine? Just for the sake of it, can you imagine such a tree? A tree that rises from your heart with its roots in your heart, and it expands to occupy the entire universe. If you really want to know the Truth of this tree or if you really want to enjoy the juice of this tree, what is more advisable? Keep running behind the whole expanse, or come straight to the root that is so near to you?

Spirituality seems quite smart. Or are spiritual people actually as dumb as we think them to be? Spirituality is smartness. It is a much wiser and efficient way of going through the business of life.

Everything that you will ever run after is actually arising from within you, in a way to bring you back to yourself. But if you keep running after that thing, then you will totally forget why you want that thing. In expressing your admiration for the fruit, you probably do not realize that you are actually worshipping the root. But if you are to worship the root, why don't you directly worship it? That is far more sensible.

Anything in the world that you want, you actually want it just to come to a final satisfaction. And if you don't come to it, you will keep wanting. That final satisfaction is called the root, *Īśā*.

So, how much to consume? *Tena tyaktena bhuñjīthā*. Only as much as is needed to go to the root. That's the principle.

How to know how much one needs in life in material terms? How much does one need in life? You could either ask a lot—in case you are chasing the leaves because the leaves are infinite, and the leaves are from here till there, from the sky till the earth. The leaves are everywhere. If you are a leaf chaser, then you will require infinite resources. You will require a lot of contacts, relationships, time, money, everything, energy, won't you? And you will keep asking for more and more resources because you are chasing the great spread of your own projection. You will be chasing so much, and then you will be requiring so much to chase it.

You will say, 'I need another one million rupees. The next thing that I am chasing is somewhere in Finland—and it is quite an expensive affair—so can I have a million more bucks, please, so that I can go chasing?'

The verse is telling us exactly how much money we need. First thing: *Mā gṛdhaḥ*. Don't covet, don't desire a lot. You do need something, but you need only as much as is needed to go within. That should decide the upper limit of your material requirement and the upper limit of your consumption. That much you must surely earn, that much you must surely obtain for yourself.

Having said that, the seer is again mischievously smiling. He is saying, 'But that much you will anyway get from Him.' *Tena tyaktena bhuñjīthā*. 'So, son, you require very little, and this little that you require you don't have to worry about earning. This much you will get as a gift from Him, provided your honest and sole objective is Him.'

That is a big catch, it is a big condition. Otherwise, you will turn lazy. Otherwise, you will say, 'First of all, I don't need to earn anything, and the little that I anyway need to have will be provided to me by the skies.' No, that is not the intention here.

What is being said is: You devote yourself relentlessly to your one pure and absolute objective, and if you do that, then the little resources—or a little more than little resources that you need to fulfil your objectives—will come from That.

Tena tyaktena. He will give. He will give you mysteriously. But that does not mean that you are being relieved from striving or working. Instead, you are being commanded to fully devote yourself to your one central desire and responsibility. Do that and you will get what you need for your work or your mission.

See, you could imagine it like this. So, we have our organization. There is this question: The donations that come to the organization come so that we perform a certain noble work, right? The ones who donate to our work, they donate so that you can bring the scriptures, light, and wisdom to more and more people. That is the reason people are supporting and contributing to our work, right?

Now, let's say, one of us walks up to a seer and asks the same question. 'Father, how much can I personally consume?' And the sage, the father will reply, *'Tena tyaktena bhuñjīthā.'* That's the reply. Put in everything into your mission, and then whatsoever is left—*tyaktena*, or *'parityakta'*, the leftover, whatsoever is the leftover—that much you can eat. If after spending everything that is needed to take the mission forward, if something is left, that you can consume. Do you get the import of this verse?

Now, I constructed this example around the theme of responsibility. I can construct a similar example around the theme of love.

Let's say, I cook something for thirty people. And, let's say, somebody is cooking along with me, and then the person who is cooking along with me asks me, 'How much do I personally consume? We have been cooking and cooking since the last three hours for thirty people, but how much do I personally consume?' And then, what do I reply? '*Tena tyaktena bhuñjīthā.* Give to everybody, and then if something is left, you can take it.' That happens in our kitchen, right? And often, after you have given everything to everybody, you find that your hunger is no more there. Then you don't even feel like consuming anything.

That's the way of life the seer is teaching the student. *Tena tyaktena bhuñjīthā.* If something is left, you take it, but do not claim anything as a matter of right. You don't have a right over everything; only the Truth has a right over everything. It all belongs to That—*Īśā vāsyamidam sarvam.* Who are you to claim anything? Nobody has any rights here. Your only right is to strive for your liberation. You strive for your liberation, and in the process, if something is left over, take it. If nothing is left over, happily go to sleep! Don't complain.

So, how should the cook's plate look like? First of all, the cook should be eating the last of all, as has been the tradition in India. If you are cooking, then you should be the last one to partake in the meals. Only after everybody has eaten will you touch the food.

Similarly, in our organization, how do you take your personal salaries? Ensure that the mission gets as much as it needs, and a little more than that. And after that, if something is left over, then you can take a little bit out of it. That should be the last item to be distributed. What? The personal things, the personal moneys. And if the mind says, 'But I have worked, and where is, you know, my remuneration?' immediately tell yourself: *Mā gṛdhaḥ*, don't covet. It is not yours. *Īśā vāsyamidam' sarvam.* It doesn't belong to you. The moneys didn't come to you so that you may personally consume them. The moneys came to you so that they can be spent in furthering the mission. Remember this.

Similarly, all this that has been given to us, it is a donation, is it not? This life is a big fat chunk of donation. You haven't earned it, it is a donation. And it has been given to you with the trust that you will make right use of it. Just as when somebody donates to us the trust is that you will make right use of it, similarly this life has been given as donation. It has been donated to you, and your responsibility is to make right use of it.

Now, how much of my life do I spend in personal gratification? What does the father say? *Tena tyaktena bhuñjīthā.* In your entire day, after doing everything that is possible for the right work, if you get, let's say, ten minutes as spare, then you can probably spend those ten minutes in your personal gratification. But only those ten minutes. *Mā gṛdhaḥ*—don't ask for more.'

This verse is then a philosophy of life. It tells you everything that you really need to know.

Anything in the world that you want, you actually want it just to come to a final satisfaction. And if you don't come to it, you will keep wanting.

40

Remember the Deed!
Remember the Deed!

Upanishad Samagam, BodhSthal, 2020

Unless you attend to the past, learn clearly from it, your past will just rename itself as your future. Actually, there is no future; it is just the past returning to you in another name, and that's the punishment you get for not learning from the past, for not remembering the past.

~

वायुरनिलममृतमथेदं भस्मांतं शरीरम् ।
ॐ क्रतो स्मर कृतं स्मर क्रतो स्मर कृतं स्मर ॥

My breath (vāyu) to immortal air: This body has ended in ashes.
Aum! Will, remember! Remember the deed! Will, remember! Remember the deed!

—Ishavasya Upanishad, Verse 17

~

Acharya Prashant (AP): This body is made of finite, mortal, earthly elements. What happens to this body and where this body comes from is no secret at all. This body comes from other bodies and all the bodies arise from the soil, just as all

272

pots arise from the soil. And who does not know what fate each of these pots meet?

The soil carries no specific form. When it takes the form of a pot, then it assumes a particular name and individuality, but that name and individuality are just playthings for a little while. Sooner than later, the pot again meets the same earth, and the pot and the earth become indistinguishable.

This is the peaceful, silent realization that the Upanishad is offering in this verse.

Remember the futility of this body. Remember how misplaced is your belief in anything valuable that can emerge from body-identification.

Please understand.

What is it that we say? 'I, who am the body, will achieve this. I, as the body, will reach there. I, who am the body, will amass wealth.'

Whatsoever we want to do, we want to do as the body, whereas the body is just earth waiting to meet the earth. It is not even waiting to meet the earth; it is already just earth, soil.

Time as an intermediary, time as an illusion, has deceived us. We think we walk on the earth. No, there is just the earth. It is not as if you are walking on the earth, it is not as if you have stepped on the soil. There is just the soil—soil on soil.

You remember Baba Bulleh Shah? 'There is just soil on soil. *Maati kudam karendi yaar.*'

And that is why I say that the Upanishads are the source of all spirituality, irrespective of place, time, or a particular branch of religion. Upanishads are the very core of religion—religion without any name, not any particular religion.

Upanishads are the very heart of religiousness itself.

Now, from this heart a lot of streams can emerge, and those streams will have names. Irrespective of what the name of the religious stream is, at its heart sit the Upanishads, irrespective of where that stream was flowing. That stream could have been that of the Ganges in the alluvial plains of India. That stream could have been the Yellow River in China. That stream could have been the Tenu, or that stream could even have been a desert river in the sands of Arabia. At its heart lie the Upanishads.

Therefore, if one has not studied the Upanishads, it will be very difficult to understand religion at all—any religion. Equally, if one resonates with the Upanishads, one will be able to appreciate all religions, any and every religion. Because all the streams, all the religious streams, whenever they flew and wherever they came from, they all have the same heart. The outer characteristics are different; the heart is the same.

You know, your hand definitely looks very different from your legs and your eyes surely do not look the same as your ears, yet they are powered by the same heart, are they not? Same is the case with all religious extensions. That which we call as religions are not really religions; they are religious streams. They could be called as extensions of the one unified body of religion itself.

So, religion is a body. One particular religion you can call as its arm, one you can call as its nose—depends on your mood. Whatsoever is the stream, the power is coming from the Upanishads. Or you could say that the power is most neatly expressed in the Upanishads. Therefore, the Upanishads are a must if you are a genuine seeker of the Truth.

So, that's what the body is all about. And all our life we have been just glorifying the body itself, right? 'I am your friend.' The moment I say that, what has actually been put on a pedestal? The body. 'I am a body, you are a body.' Now friendship is a side affair. The central thing is that I have considered you and me as a body.

'I am your wife' or 'I am your husband'—what is the foremost and central assertion here? 'You are a body, I am a body.'

Whatever we have done, we have just done as bodies. Even to God, when we have prayed, we have prayed as bodies. 'Oh, my God, I have just come to your church or your temple or your mosque!' You have come to a mosque? Now, Truth doesn't move. What has come to some place? Obviously, the limited body, the 70 kilograms that you call as yourself. 'This is me! This 70 kg is me, and I have come to the temple!'

So, the Upanishad says—and it is beautiful:

'Oṃ, krato smara kṛtaṃ smara, krato smara kṛtaṃ smara.'

Remember the doer, remember the deeds; remember the doer, remember the deeds.

This body is not you, and yet whatever you have done, you have done as the body!

Oṃ, krato smara kṛtam' smara. Remember the doer, remember the deed; remember the doer, remember the deed.

If you can just take away this much: remember, remember, remember! The Upanishads are not saying, 'Forget your past and enjoy the present.' The Upanishads are emphasizing again and again, 'Look at the repetition! Krato smara kṛtam' smara, krato smara kṛtam' smara. Don't forget, don't ever forget what you have been doing all your life. All your life you have been making the central mistake, and the central mistake is to think that life belongs to the body. The central mistake is to think that the body lives.'

Tell me, tell me. *(Referring to people in the audience)* I mean, he's your friend, right? Had he had no consciousness, how valuable would he be to you?

Q: Valueless.

AP: Why? The body is the same.

You are attracted to a woman, let's say. If her consciousness distorts, how valuable does she remain to you? I am not even talking of an absence of consciousness; I am talking of just distorted consciousness. Does she remain valuable to you? And yet we behave as if the body is the real thing.

Had the body been the real thing, then you would have continued to preserve the body even after death. And today, you have scientific, medical means to preserve the body for a really long time. Those means were there even in the days of the mummies, and today those means are far more advanced. You can preserve the body. Would you do that?

Your best friend passes away. Would you preserve the body? Why not? You are the body, your friend is the body, and the body can be preserved. Why don't you preserve the body? But that appears so stupid! If that appears so stupid, then *krato smara kṛtam˙ smara.*

Remember, this is what you did to your friend all his life, all your life. You have looked at him just as the body. Have you bothered to really know his real name? His real name is consciousness; his real name is the little self, the ego. I call it *atript caitanya.* That's what our one, shared, common name is—the real name. We all are unfulfilled consciousness.

But is that how we look at each other? No. We look at each other as bodies. And that is even more tempting if the other body is alluring, belongs to the other gender, or is alluring in some other way.

The body is of, let's say, your little kid. Then it becomes even more difficult to look at your kid as actually consciousness in motion. You care for his body—do you care so much for his consciousness? Really not. The kid comes to you, the kid is hungry, and that will disturb you, right? But what if the kid is really hungry from within? Do you even detect that?

The kid returns from the playground, it is evening time. There is a scratch on his leg, and you will be alerted: 'Oh, what is it? Where did you get it from? Let me clean the wound. Let me put some medicine on it.' What if there is a mark on his consciousness, on his mind? Are you worried even a little bit? There is a little scratch on the body and an alarm is raised— and so many scratches on the mind and nobody bothers!

That's what must be remembered. That's what we have done throughout, and that's what we are not to do any further.

Oṃ, krato smara krtam˙smara, krato smara krtam˙smara.

The past is a great resource; it is not to be wasted away or thrown away or forgotten. If you do not really decode your past, you are bound to repeat it. If you have not been able to unravel your past, then you will simply relive your past.

So, forget all the propaganda coming from the neo-spiritual circles that say that the past is something to be just kept aside and you have to move on and life is in the present, so what will you do with the past?

Go back, return to the past again and again. Why must you return to the past again and again? Because your fundamental tendencies have not changed. So, when you are returning to the past, you are actually looking at yourself as you are right now.

You cannot look at yourself as you are right now because in this moment there is no space, no allowance for that. So, how will you know who you are? You are someone who hasn't really changed. Very few people really manage to transcend their old self.

So, who are you? You are much the same as you were two years back. So, how do you know yourself? Just look at what you did two years back. That's exactly what is happening in your life right now. Worse still, that is also what is waiting to happen tomorrow.

Unless you attend to the past, learn clearly from it, your past will just rename itself as your future.

Actually, there is no future; it is just the past returning to you in another name, and that's the punishment you get for not learning from the past, for not remembering the past.

Therefore, the Upanishad is saying, '*Oṃ, krato smara kṛtaṃ smara, krato smara kṛtaṃ smara.*' And do that again and again.

See how the cycle is operating within you. See how you are much the same as you were at the age of five. See how only the external stuff has changed. See how the inner tendencies have just not evolved or sublimated.

Time as an intermediary, time as an illusion, has deceived us. We think we walk on the earth. No, there is just the earth. It is not as if you are walking on the earth, it is not as if you have stepped on the soil. There is just the soil—soil on soil.

PrashantAdvait Foundation

PrashantAdvait Foundation (PAF) is a non-profit socio-spiritual organization founded and led by Acharya Prashant. It was established with an objective to demolish falseness—both within the human being, and in the society in general—and promote a scientific and spiritual attitude towards self and life.

How does the Foundation operate?

The Foundation facilitates Acharya Prashant's discourses on various platforms and organizes spiritual retreats, online courses, lectures and conferences. Over the years, Acharya Prashant has spoken upon more than fifty Vedantic scriptures. Beyond Upanishads and Gitas, Acharya Prashant has spoken on several other saints, sages and topics of timeless essence.

These discourses are recorded and tuned into educational courses, so that they reach as many as possible in the most organized form.

Where is the content available?

a. **Mobile App:** Even as Acharya Prashant continues to generate his literature and commentaries at a prolific rate, the Foundation's role lies in collating, documenting and publishing everything in a form that preserves the original nature of the works for the centuries ahead. In the most organized form, Acharya Prashant's courses and books have been stored for public use at the Foundation's official mobile app. This app has been created as a timeless source of pure knowledge for all those who will ever seek the Truth.

b. **Website:** Acharya Prashant's courses and books are also available at the Foundation's website: www.solutions. acharyaprashant.org

c. **Social Media:** Acharya Prashant's channels on YouTube, Facebook, Instagram, Twitter, etc. all carry huge volumes of educational content for all, and are managed by the Foundation.

Sections most benefitted by the Foundation's work:

a. **Non-human life forms** including animals and plants: Given that the overwhelmingly biggest threat to flora and fauna of all kind comes from the ignorance of man about his own body and self, reforming man's mind is the best way to save nature. It is estimated that millions of animals especially animals used for food – chicken, goat, sheep, cows, buffaloes, fish have been saved due to Acharya Prashant's work. Besides, a large number of wild animals too have been saved. With his efforts over the years, it is estimated that lakhs, if not millions, of people have adopted vegetarianism or veganism and have chosen an awakened lifestyle involving environmental consciousness and a low carbon footprint. Many see him as the spiritual face of the vegan movement.

b. **Youth**: Youth, especially in India, face multi-directional challenges coming from the conditioning acquired from family, society, education and media, career challenges, dilemmas about physicality, love and relationships and deep existential questions about the meaning and purpose of life. They are in delicate situation where the chances of making suboptimal decisions and life taking unhealthy turns are quite high. Acharya Prashant has been unique in addressing the energy and conflicts of the youth. There are so may who remain indebted to him for having received lifesaving clarity at critical junctures of decision making.

c. **Women**: Women throughout the world, and especially in India, continue to be recognized as the largely disempowered half of mankind. While there have been concerted efforts in the social, political, economic ways to instil women with due agency and power, yet nothing is really effective without the inner dimension of clarity and freedom. Acharya Prashant's work has been to awaken women to their true identity beyond the compulsions of the body and the conditioning of the mind. Countless women today—from the teenage schoolgirl to the septuagenarian homemaker—owe their sense of liberty and clarity, and the courage to rise against external oppression and internal debilitation, to the teachings of the master.

d. **Spiritual seekers**: There is a large class of spiritual seekers for whom spirituality is a not much more than entertainment. Then there are those for whom spirituality is a respectable name for medieval superstition. Then those who come to spirituality to escape the bare realities of life. Then those who suppose that spirituality consists of esoteric rituals, methods, and exercises. Then those who want only superficial treatments to deep underlying life problems. Acharya Prashant has been well known to vigorously shake all such seekers out of their self-deceptive psychic stupor. And then there is the odd genuine seeker. The one who has already tried hard to go into the recesses of his mind, and the reality of life. The one who is prepared to work hard for his liberation. The one who is fed up of self-imposed bondages, and is prepared to pay the price for freedom. Acharya Prashant comes as a rare and real friend to such seekers.

Over the years more and more volunteers from various fields of life have joined the Foundation, working relentlessly to help spread the Teachings. Today, the Foundation has touched and affected the lives of more than ten million individuals, and these numbers are only going to multiply in the coming times.

To know more about the Foundation, visit acharyaprashant.org. To learn about the Foundation's courses, visit solutions. acharyaprashant.org. To contact the Foundation, email at requests@advait.org.in